Visions of the Future

Socialist History 15

Edited by
Willie Thompson,
David Parker, Mike Waite,
David Morgan and
Heather Williams

Rivers Oram Press
London, Sydney and New York

Editorial Team
Willie Thompson
David Parker
Mike Waite
David Morgan
Kevin Morgan
Heather Williams
Stephen Woodhams

Editorial Advisors
Noreen Branson
Rodney Hilton
Eric Hobsbawm
David Howell
Monty Johnstone
Victor Kiernan
David Marquand
Ben Pimlott
Pat Thane

Published in 1999
by Rivers Oram Press, an imprint of Rivers Oram Publishers Ltd
144 Hemingford Road, London N1 1DE

Distributed in the USA by
New York University Press
838 Broadway
New York, NY 10003-482

Distributed in Australia and New Zealand by
UNIReps
University of New South Wales
Sydney, NSW 2052

Set in Garamond by
NJ Design Associates, Romsey, Hants
and printed in Great Britain by
T.J.International Ltd, Padstow, Cornwall

This edition copyright © 1999 Socialist History Society
The articles are copyright © 1999 David Burke, Philip Coupland, Fred Lindop, David Purdy, Maureen Speller, Willie Thompson

No part of this journal may be produced in any form, except for the quotation of brief passages in criticism, without the written permission of the publishers. The right of the contributors to be identified as the authors has been asserted by them in accordance with the Copyright, Designs and Patents Act 1988

British Library Cataloguing in Publication Data
A catalogue record for this publication is available from the British Library
ISBN 1 85489 114 6 (hb)
ISBN 1 85489 115 4 (pb)
ISSN 0969 4331

Contents

Editorial   v
The insignificance of the millennium

Utopianism   1
David Purdy

'Utopia' in British Political Culture   17
The desire that dare not speak its name
Philip Coupland

The Way the Future Was   33
Maureen Speller

Theodore Rothstein and the Origins of the British Communist Party   45
David Burke and Fred Lindop

Socialist History: A personal note   66
Willie Thompson

Reviews
Nineteenth-century millennium   69
Edward Royle, *Robert Owen and the Commencement of the Millennium: A Study of the Harmony Community*

Religion, Labour and the New Jerusalem   74
Robert Pope, *Building Jerusalem: Nonconformity, Labour and the Social Question in Wales, 1906–1939*

Women's suffrage 76
Maroula Joannou and June Purvis (eds), *The Women's Suffrage Movement: New Feminist Perspectives*

Revolutionary encyclopaedia 78
Edward Acton, Vladimir Iu. Cherniaev and William G. Rosenberg (eds), *Critical Companion to the Russian Revolution 1914–1921*

The general staff of the world revolution 82
Tim Rees and Andrew Thorpe (eds), *International Communism and the Communist International 1919–43*

Mystery man 85
R. Darlington, *The Political Trajectory of J. T. Murphy*
M. Murphy, *Molly Murphy: Suffragette and Socialist*

Culture and the future that never was 89
Andy Croft (ed.), *A Weapon in the Struggle: The cultural history of the Communist Party in Britain*
David Margolies (ed.), *Writing the Revolution: Cultural criticism from Left Review*
J. Hoberman, *The Red Atlantis: Communist culture in the absence of communism*

Books Received 93

Conference Report 95
Mike Tyldesley and Laurence Cox

Editorial

The insignificance of the millennium

This issue of *Socialist History* has been put together against the backdrop of preparations for millennium 'celebrations', of which the most significant in Britain will be the opening of the Greenwich Dome. The reasoning behind the Labour government's early decision to push ahead with the project, inherited from the previous Tory administration, seems to have centred on the idea that the Dome could be an opportunity to project and popularise a vision of a modernising and optimistic Britain; a country renewing itself in line with the self-image the Labour leadership had of itself as the creator of a new kind of political project, shaped by and shaping the circumstances of these times.

It is interesting, then, that there has been so much uncertainty and so little coherence about what the Dome should contain and present. The combination of secrecy and partial unveilings of plans which marked late 1998 and much of 1999 may have been part of a clever marketing plan. On the other hand, the resignations of key officials and politicians, crises over sponsorship, and shapeless debates over such issues as how Dome exhibits could address 'spirituality', and Christianity in particular, suggest that the organising principle of the 'millennium experience' which visitors to Greenwich will enjoy and endure will be the absence of a coherent vision of how Britain is and how it could be as 1999 becomes 2000.

It cannot be entirely fair to blame the government for the non-coincidence of such a vision and new year 2000. To speak of the dawn of the millennium is, after all, merely a way of naming a moment which comes about as a necessary consequence of conceptions of time constructed long ago, without any reference to the patterns and dynamics of contemporary social life. The date does not even correspond to divisions in time which have to do with the cycles resulting from the realities of the earth's movement.

Why, then, are people being asked to attach such significance to the moment, as something which should have unique meaning, as a time when something should happen, as a day which will be marked by celebrations and levels of hype which will be hard to stomach?

One of the things that is happening is a confusion between two very different ways of thinking about time - cyclical time and linear time. For much of human history, time seems to have been conceived of in terms of cycles. Birth, life, death. The pattern of seasons. The moments of solstice. Sowing and reaping. Such realities patterned a way of thinking about beginnings and endings in which things came back to a starting point over and over again. Anthony Giddens has reminded us that 'for mast of human history, the most striking thing is constancy rather than change. Only at a certain period, relatively recent in historical time, is there an injection of dynamism into history.'[1]

Perhaps the most important contribution to forming the idea of counting the moments of time in a linear way, starting from a once-only event and then proceeding in cumulative series into the indefinite future, has come from Christian theology. This tradition has preserved the cyclical image of time, whilst introducing alongside it the notion of linear progression conceived as a path of salvation whose final meaning would be determined on Judgement Day, at the end of history. To set this conception alongside the experienced realities of life an earth, Christian ideologists carefully set up the linear time calculations which worked back to the imagined moment of Christ's birth, and thus provided the mechanisms for naming the moments which now count us down to eve-of-millennium parties. The round number-moment 2000 sounds as if it should be significant because it suggests that we're returning to a new starting point, and that some kind of clock has gone round full circle so that we can begin again. In reality, the date is no more significant than any other automatic consequence of counting in a cumulative sequence.

That the millennium is, in this sense, insignificant can be underlined by reminding ourselves that a calendar derived from Christianity does not hold central importance for many millions of people—even if the domination of American and 'western' powers have established that calendar as a global reference paint. It must also be acknowledged that various conceptions of time, cycles, and new beginnings also play an important part in the way that followers of other major world religions such as Islam conceive their place in the world.

In other ways, though, we must recognise that conceptions such as that of the significance of the millennium do have some impact on the way that people think and behave. And some of this behaviour is much more consequential than the spending sprees and celebrations we'll be urged to indulge in over the new year holiday 1999/2000. As Norman Cohn argued in *The Pursuit of the Millennium*, the Christian church battled for long centuries against movements in which 'the desire of the poor to improve the material conditions of their lives became transfused with phantasies of a new Paradise on earth ... generation after generation was seized at least intermittently by a tense expectation of some sudden, miraculous event in which the world would be utterly transformed'.[2] The repeated insistence of theologians that the book of Revelation was to be understood as a spiritual allegory, and that the kingdom of heaven was an event which would take place not in space and time but only in the soul of believers, reflected the interests of a church which had become established and organised.[3] But the mobilising power of the myth of millennial and apocalyptic change was not easily undone by Council edicts and Augustinian statements.

Progress at the Millennium

Melucci, amongst others, has argued that 'modern ideas of progress and revolution are but desacralised versions of the Christian legacy' and has associated medieval conceptions of progress towards the real or spiritual millennium with nineteenth century conceptions of social development.[4]

But the transfer of patterns of thought from medieval Christianity to the modern world was mediated by new material factors. Notions of progress and social change, and the sense that 'history' had a direction towards a potentially better future, emerged from the 1700s onwards, as western societies increasingly acquired the powers to intervene on their environment and on themselves. This capacity involved an interplay between technological advance and social change, generating much thought about the extent to which the one determined and shaped the other. Scientific advance increasingly improved the lives of millions of people, and made possible the expansion in human population and increasing lifespans which are features of the world today.

But progress and social transformation have not merely been the consequence of technological breakthroughs. The modern world has been shaped by political projects which have had multiple impacts an peoples' lives, for better and for worse. Many of these, from various forms of democratic politics, civic nationalist movements and the socialist traditions, have been conceived of and justified as efforts to move on to better things.

One significant feature of the social and intellectual landscape at this turn of millennium is that this secular 'faith in progress' seems to be in as much a state of collapse and uncertainty as the religious Christianity which some would claim that it mirrors. The intellectual fashion of postmodernism, with its 'scepticism in the face of grand narratives' and its relativist tendencies, is only one expression of this crisis. The collapse of the twentieth century communist experiment, and the weakly contested accommodation of social democracy to the 'realities' of global neo-liberalism, show the current exhaustion of efforts to reshape social life through rational appraisal of the real needs of humans and of attempts to meet them through consciously determined social and technological progress. In the place of positive and confident agendas—however weak and flawed the actual projects which came from then were—we now live in a world in which the most dynamic political movements are shaped by the ferocious hatreds of oppressive ethnic nationalisms, or the reactionary impulses of religious fundamentalism.

Other social movements have reacted against the 'benefits' of technology and are voicing scepticism about its value. Green politics have grown from the recognition that technological progress is having serious environmental consequences; whilst the notion that the environment is something to be 'mastered' is now increasingly seen to be problematic. Speculation about the dawning of the millennium centres not only an the question of where the best parties will be, but also on the possible consequences of the 'millennium bug', and the potential breakdown of everything, from international banking to domestic microwave ovens, which depends on computer chips. As the Home Secretary spends his New Year's eve in some Whitehall emergency planning bunker, anticipating what form 'datapanik in the year zero' might take, perhaps we will begin to reflect on why technology, which has been developed to help us shape and use the world around us, so often turns out to have unintended consequences and to elude our control.[5]

Visions of the Future—The Contents of Issue 15

In order to construct a convincing and practical politics which draws on the best of enlightenment and democratic traditions, whilst tempering the urge to 'conquer' nature with a recognition that human social life must operate in respectful interaction with the environment, an ongoing critical assessment of past efforts at political progress is necessary. The first major article in this issue of *Socialist History* suggests that imagining alternative futures is also essential. Mechanisms to contrast the realities of how things are with conceptions of the ways things should be are central tools of any political movements for change. David Purdy offers an interpretation of the utopian tradition which comments on recent contributions to utopian studies; draws a sharp distinction between utopian speculation and political practice; demarcates utopianism from both realism and fantasy; and argues for the abiding importance of utopian speculation as a tool of moral and intellectual enquiry.

Philip Coupland further explores the nature of utopianism, with a study of the ways in which utopian political language was mobilised and used on the British left in the 1930s.

Maureen Spellar provides an overview of the genre of science fiction, focusing in particular on the work of British and American writers. Whilst sci-fi might seem at first glance to be the imaginative exploration of the possible consequences of technological and scientific advance, Spellar shows how, in common with utopian political thought, it has often served as a way of imagining and exploring other possible social formations. She also emphasises how particular works of sci-fi were influenced and shaped by the social trends and realities through which the authors were living.

One of the most self-consciously 'progressive' political movements in history has been the twentieth century communist movement. David Burke and Fred Lindop focus on the contribution of Theodore Rothstein to the establishment of organised communism in Britain, in an article which looks at the left milieu after the first world war, and raises questions about the balances between domestic impulses and Russian influence in the setting up of the Communist Party of Great Britain.

Themes from these articles are picked up in the book reviews section. Gregory Claeys provides a substantial assessment of a most influential 'utopian', focusing on one of Robert Owen's experiments in social living.

A group of reviews address different aspects of the communist project. Heather Williams assesses a collection of papers an the Communist International, the world-wide organisation set up to promote and apply revolutionary politics in all countries. John Callaghan reviews a biography of one of the British communists who served as an official of the Comintern. And Geoff Andrews reviews books which look at ways the communist movement related to and influenced cultural life and production.

Other contributions to this issue of *Socialist History* pick up its main themes in different ways; these range from accounts of a Manchester conference series which considers how conceptions of 'alternative futures' fuel and resource contemporary social movements, to book reviews on the women's suffrage movement and on the interaction between a Christian church and politics in Wales.

The Socialist History Editorial Team

A number of changes in the arrangements for editing the journal will be in place from the next issue of *Socialist History*. Willie Thompson, who has been the editor of the journal since it was established, and previously edited *Our History Journal* for the Communist Party History Group, marks his standing down from this role with brief reflections on the various forms that the journal has taken.

Kevin Morgan takes over the central role of journal editor. He has written many items which may be familiar to readers, including a careful account of British left politics in the 1930s, and the biography of Harry Pollitt, as well as contributing chapters and articles to a range of collections of essays and journals.[6] Kevin can be contacted at the Department of Government, University of Manchester, N13 9PL. His e-mail address is kevin.morgan@man.ac.uk

At the same time, Stephen Woodhams, Honorary Research Fellow at Birkbeck College, London, takes over the responsibility of book reviews editor from Mike Waite. Stephen can be e-mailed at s.woodhams@polsoc.bbk.ac.uk

Kate Duffy will serve as assistant reviews editor, and will be particularly responsible for the administrative aspects of the role. She can be contacted at University of Luton, Park Square, Luton, LU1 3JU. Her e-mail address is kate.duffy@luton.ac.uk

Both Willie Thompson and Mike Waite will continue as members of the editorial team, and plans are afoot to invite others associated with socialist and labour movement history to 'guest edit' particular issues of the journal. We are confident that these changes and the expansion of the editorial team will lead to continued improvements in the quality and range of contributions and coverage, and will help the journal reach out to new audiences and readers.

The Editors

Notes

1. Anthony Giddens, in *Conversations with Anthony Giddens: Making sense of modernity*, Polity Press, Cambridge, 1998, p.91.
2. N. Cohn, *The Pursuit of the Millennium*, Secker and Warburg, London, 1957, page xiii.
3. Cohn, op cit., p.13.
4. Alberto Melucci, *Changing Codes: Collective action in the information age*, Cambridge University Press, Cambridge, 1996, p.49.
5. 'Datapanik In the Year Zero' was issued by the Cleveland-based experimental rock band Pere Ubu in 1978.
6. Kevin Morgan, *Against Fascism and War: Ruptures and continuities in British Communist politics 1935–41*, Manchester University Press, Manchester 1989; *Harry Pollitt*, Manchester University Press, Manchester 1993; 'The Communist Party and the *Daily Worker*' in Geoff Andrews, Nina Fishman and K. Morgan (eds), *Opening the Books: Essays on the social and cultural history of the British Communist Party*, Pluto Press, London 1995; 'King Street Blues: Jazz and the left in Britain in the 1930s–40s' in Andy Croft (ed.), *A Weapon in the Struggle: The cultural history of the Communist Party in Britain*, Pluto Press, London, 1998.

Socialist History Journal

The *Socialist History Journal* explores and assesses the past of the socialist movement and broader processes in relation to it, not only for the sake of historical understanding, but as an input and contribution to the movement's future development. The journal is not exclusive and welcomes argument and debate from all viewpoints.

Other *Socialist History* titles:

A Bourgeois Revolution?
Socialist History 1 · 1993
0 7453 08058

What Was Communism? Pt 1
Socialist History 2 · 1993
0 7453 08066

What Was Communism? Pt 2
Socialist History 3 · 1993
0 7453 08074

The Labour Party Since 1945
Socialist History 4 · 1994
0 7453 08082

The Left and Culture
Socialist History 5 · 1994
0 7453 08090

The Personal and the Political
Socialist History 6 · 1994
0 7453 08104

Fighting the Good Fight?
Socialist History 7 · 1995
0 7453 10613

Historiography and the British Marxist Historians
Socialist History 8 · 1995
0 7453 08120

Labour Movements
Socialist History 9 · 1996
0 7453 08139

Revisions?
Socialist History 10 · 1996
0 7453 08147

The Cold War
Socialist History 11 · 1997
0 7453 12411

Nationalism and Communist Party History
Socialist History 12 · 1997
0 7453 12675

Imperialism and Internationalism
Socialist History 13 · 1998
1 85489 1073

The Future of History
Socialist History 14 · 1998
1 85489 109X

Visions of the Future
Socialist History 15 · 1999
1 85489 1154

America
Socialist History 16 · 1999
1 85489 1170

Utopianism
David Purdy

'Utopia' was the name given by Thomas More (1965 [1516]) to an imaginary island just beyond the edge of the known world. Its inhabitants live in graceful cities of roughly equal size, each surrounded by a broad belt of farmland and forest. They practise democracy, cultivate pleasure, but despise avarice, and their moneyless economy is flourishing, but stationary. Living standards are modest, but there is strict equality in consumption and no one is poor. Work is communal and compulsory, but hours of work are short and, with certain exceptions, the division of labour is free from hierarchy. The most gifted and virtuous young people are trained to become civil servants, magistrates and priests, whilst menial tasks are performed by convicts and poor immigrants. There are also some residual inequalities between men and women. Girls are educated alongside boys and are free to enter the full range of occupations (except that on the battlefield their role is confined to cheerleading). At the same time, each household comes under the authority of the eldest male and wives are subordinate to their husbands. It is also noteworthy that while materially motivated crime is virtually unknown, human passion can still cause problems and marital infidelity is a criminal offence.

The Utopian way of life is described during a long conversation between More himself and one Raphael Hythlodaeus, a garrulous mariner recently returned from the Americas, who takes delight in contrasting the virtues of heathen Utopia with the vices of Christian Europe. The name itself is a play on the Greek words 'ou' (not), 'eu' (well, rightly) and 'topos' (place). Thus, in its original, non-derogatory sense, 'utopia' denoted a good, but non-existent society.

More's prototype was followed by a long line of successors. In the process, 'utopia' came to signify an *impossible* ideal of perfection. This pejorative connotation—perhaps conveyed more unequivocally by the adjective than by the noun—may be mildly good-humoured. But it can also be vehemently hostile. No one likes to be thought 'utopian' and people never apply this epithet to themselves.

Socialists have long used the word to abuse their opponents, though it is worth recalling that in *Socialism: Utopian and Scientific*, Engels (1970 [1892]) tempers his criticism of Fourier, Owen and Saint-Simon with praise for their insights and courage. The chief misfortune of the utopian socialists, he suggests—somewhat condescendingly—was that they set out to transform bourgeois society at a time when the proletariat was not yet mature enough to assume its predestined role as capitalism's gravedigger.

Liberals such as Popper and Hayek are fierce opponents of utopian thought, condemning the incipient totalitarianism of all attempts to prescribe a fixed and final pattern for human development. But in his restatement of liberal theory, Nozick (1974) finesses this argument. He agrees that 'freedom destroys patterns', but nevertheless proposes what he calls a 'framework for utopia'. By this he means a minimum state, the least intrusive form of political power commensurate with the defence of individual rights. People's conceptions of the good life are, he submits, extraordinarily diverse: no way of life can be ideal for everyone and no single form of social organisation is best. Nevertheless, we can still retain the *concept* of utopia provided it is re-interpreted as a libertarian framework for experiments in living. In the light of this proposal, it was somewhat ironic that when the collapse of Communism was proclaimed as the end of history, many people assumed that utopia had been wiped off the map. We are all, it seems, anti-utopians now.

Possible worlds and the art of the possible

The notion that utopias are in some way intellectually disreputable springs from misplaced literalness and a simple failure to distinguish between 'should' and 'shall'. Suppose that instead of criticising actually existing social arrangements, I want to form some idea of what a good society might look like. One way for me to proceed is to frame some standard of excellence and then to visualise in my mind's eye, and with as much attention to detail and plausibility as I can manage, a social order that measures up to it. This by no means obliges me to take any view, one way or the other, about the quite separate question as to how, if at all, such a society might be brought into existence. Still less does it commit me to urging the pursuit of my ideal at any price. After all, what is best in the abstract may not be what is best *all things considered*, taking due account of cultural inertia, political dynamics and the irreducible uncertainty that surrounds all but the most immediate consequences of our actions.

If utopian thinkers themselves have not always respected these distinctions, it was not because they were fanatics bent on realising the ideal society at all costs. More often, they have been political innocents, unshakeably convinced that they had unriddled the universe and fondly imagining that a grateful humanity was about to acclaim their discoveries and proceed forthwith to inaugurate an era of universal peace, contentment and justice. This essentially religious conception, grounded in revealed truth, is certainly part of the utopian tradition. Charles Fourier, described by his biographer as 'the nineteenth century's complete utopian', offers a perfect case in point (Beecher, 1986). But a flawed reality principle is far from characteristic of the tradition as whole.

Naive salvationism does, to be sure, contain what Kumar (1991) calls the 'archetypes' or formative themes of utopia: the element of *harmony* represented by the myth of an original Golden Age or Earthly Paradise; the element of *hope* encapsulated by the Judaeo-Christian belief in the Millennium; the element of *design* reflected in the Renaissance ideal of the Perfect City; and the element of *bliss*, defined as the absence of unsatisfied desire and variously conceived: as cornucopia in popular fantasy; as Nirvana in spiritual teaching; and as a state of calm felicity in humanist ethics. But archetypes are precisely primordial forms awaiting further development. Images of harmony, hope, design and bliss predate More's *Utopia*. They even predate Plato's *Republic* which served More both as a model and as a foil. And they continue to permeate the utopian tradition. But they are not what typifies utopian thought. These images can also be found, for example, in fairy tales, propaganda and song.

Exactly what distinguishes utopia from other essays in creative imagination is considered shortly. The point to be noted here is simply that utopia is not a political programme. Utopian thinkers make a more or less conscious effort to disengage the sociological imagination from the art of politics. They step back from the flux of time and chance in order to visualise as clearly as possible what the best, or at any rate a very much better, society would look like *if* it could somehow be achieved, and even if they themselves are strongly inclined to doubt it, as More, for example, certainly was.

Just *why* anyone should want to speculate about possible worlds that may never come to pass is also taken up later. But whatever the reason, this *is* what utopian writers do. More's punning name for the ideal society already indicates as much. So too does his use of the traveller's tale as a way of 'getting to' utopia and reporting back on the experience. The dialogue form reinforces this device. It also enables More to distance himself from his interlocutor's enthusiasm for all things utopian, striking a sceptical note about the prospect of founding a comparable state in Europe. Subsequent utopias employ similar methods of inducing the suspension of belief. As the planet is compassed and charted, the voyage of discovery is replaced by the journey through space or time. For William Morris (1970 [1891]) utopian exploration is all in the mind: *News from Nowhere* purports to recount a dream he had after a particularly argumentative meeting of the Hammersmith Socialist Party!

The separation of long-range vision from time-bound action explains why pictures of utopia are so often lifeless and dull. They may, as William Morris hoped, promote the 'education of desire'. But they can also elicit profound ennui. Images of paradise, in this life or the next, moved William James (1897: 168) to complain:

> If this be the whole fruit of the victory ... if the generations of mankind suffered and laid down their lives; if prophets confessed and martyrs sang in the fire and all the sacred tears were shed for no other end than that a race of creatures of such unexampled insipidity should succeed, and protract *in saecula saeculorum* their contented and inoffensive lives, why, at such a rate, better lose than win the battle, or at all events better ring down the curtain before the last act of the play, so that a business that began so importantly may be saved from so singularly flat a winding up.

Mapping utopia

Students of utopia dispute its proper definition. Some simply evade the issue. The Manuels, for example, offer an encyclopaedic 'history' of utopia without ever explaining, let alone justifying, the principles guiding their selection of material (Manuel and Manuel, 1979). This is clearly unsatisfactory.

Levitas (1990) confronts the issue squarely, but rejects definitions based on some alleged common content, form or function as too restrictive. The range of utopian endeavour, she insists, extends to all expressions of the desire for better ways of living and being. But this definition is surely not restrictive enough. On the one hand, it includes aspirations which are wholly unrealistic, not in the contingent sense that they are unlikely to be satisfied given the prevailing balance of social and political power, but in the more fundamental sense that they conflict with permanent and unalterable features of human nature or the human condition. This, I shall argue later, obliterates the distinction between utopia and fantasy. On the other hand, not every aspiration for a better way of living which could, in principle, be realised, automatically qualifies as utopian. In *Walden*, for example, Thoreau (1977 [1854]) describes an 'experiment in political economy' designed to demonstrate just how little we need to be happy. The simple life that he recommends is perfectly feasible: he is, after all, writing from first-hand experience. But he does not discuss, and perhaps has no wish to discuss, the implications of his precepts for the organisation of society as a whole. His vision of the good life is utterly solitary. The classical utopia, by contrast, aims to show not just what kind of life is best, but also what kinds of social arrangements are needed to sustain it.

Kumar (op.cit.) avoids these difficulties, without in any way limiting the scope of utopian studies, by emphasising what he calls the 'utopian tradition', and by distinguishing different forms of utopian thought. The concept of utopia, he argues, is bounded in space and time. It draws, as we saw earlier, on ancient archetypes. But the utopian tradition proper originated in early modern Europe as one expression of Renaissance humanism.

There might conceivably be a case for saying that it was Plato who invented the concept of utopia, even though it was More who gave it a name. But Kumar rejects this view. In the 'Republic' Plato is centrally concerned with the good life, but only incidentally with the good society, and not at all with the connections between them. Socrates holds that the good life—which he takes to mean the life of the just or virtuous man—can be lived in any kind of society. Admittedly, much of the 'Republic' is given over to a discourse on the nature of the just state. But this is a digression from the original inquiry into the nature of moral virtue prompted by the insistence of Thrasymachus that 'Justice is the interest of the stronger'. To make it easier for his listeners to grasp the *concept* of justice, Socrates, invites them to consider how it might be applied to the large-scale case of society as a whole. The just state, he eventually concludes, requires harmonious co-operation between functionally specialised classes under the rule of the Guardians. By analogy, the just man is one who maintains a proper balance between appetite, will and reason, but keeps reason in overall command.

Certainly, Socrates believes that the state will not be just unless it is ruled by a disinterested intellectual elite who have renounced all personal possessions and family ties. But he explicitly denies that it is impossible to live a just life unless one lives in a just state. This is not the position taken by More's raconteur. His survey of Utopian customs and institutions leaves no doubt that, in secular matters at least, good people are only to be found in a good society. Moreover, Plato considers only the rulers of the Republic: their subjects are expected to display submission, not virtue. By contrast, *all* Utopia's citizens share equally in the benefits and burdens of social life (though not all its denizens are citizens).

If Plato's *Republic* was pre-utopian in its concerns, there is another, later type of social thought which stands outside the utopian canon, but which nevertheless shares the similar preoccupations and premises. Utopianism is not confined to a literary genre: it also includes what Kumar (op.cit.) calls 'utopian theory'. Writers such as Rousseau and Marx did not produce 'speaking pictures' of the good society. Indeed, Marx disdained to write 'recipes for the cookbooks of the future'. But he can still be regarded as a 'utopian theorist' in so far as he outlines a general framework for thinking about an ideal, or better, form of society. No doubt the founders of 'scientific socialism' would have retorted that ethical ideals are a form of ideology: social in origin, illusory in content and serving class interests. Yet their own work abounds in moral judgements and is clearly fired by the desire to create a better world. Moreover, as was pointed out earlier, their disagreement with the utopian socialists was about how capitalism was to be replaced by socialism: they were not necessarily averse to speculation about the future as such. And their vision of communism, like Rousseau's vision of a self-governing city-state, displays a strong family resemblance to the classical utopias. The 'higher stage' of communism is a form of human association in which:

(1) ownership and control of the means of production have been socialised (which is not, incidentally, the same as concentrating ownership in the hands of the state and creating a command economy);
(2) antagonisms rooted in the social division of labour have been overcome by breaking down the separation between mental and manual labour, removing the gulf between town and country, and ending the sexual division of labour;
(3) progressive reductions in working time, the expansion of free time and improvements in the quality of working life have transformed work from a toilsome necessity into life's prime want;
(4) there being no further need for either legal compulsion or economic incentives to motivate contributions to social production, the distribution of income is governed by the principle: 'From each according to his ability to each according to his needs';
(5) since the social structure is no longer distorted by class and other sources of systematic social inequality, people no longer experience and relate to each other as dominants, subordinates and rivals; conversely, since people have acquired the capacity, opportunity and desire to take responsibility both for their own lives and for the natural and social

environment which they share with others, the polity is organised a partnership between free and equal citizens.

Notice that communism is described here as if it had already been achieved: as if, that is, humanity had already passed through the indefinitely long, anterior process of social learning and development generically known as socialism or the 'lower stage' of communism. The trick of looking backward from an imaginary future is characteristic of utopian thought: its favourite tense is the future perfect. It would, however, make just as much sense to describe communism from the opposite perspective, looking forward from the reality of the present. In this case, what stands out is the immensity of the gulf between the communist ideal and the world as it is. The intervening process of social evolution now appears as an aspiration, a challenge or a hopeless cause, according to one's judgement. Either way, whether the *status quo* comes first or last, one can think of a fully developed communist society as the limiting point in a series of ever more radical social transformations, every one of which is entirely hypothetical. The significance of this conception will emerge in due course.

Utopia as thought experiment

I have argued that utopianism is a form of social thought; that it includes both fiction and theory; and that it occupies the space between realism and fantasy. The first two of these points have been sufficiently discussed already. The bounds of utopia call for further definition.

What is it that distinguishes utopian thought from social realism? Consider works of fiction. In the typical realist novel, interest centres on character, plot or atmosphere. To disguise the fact that these are all products of her imagination, the writer situates them within a 'realistic' social and historical setting which her readers will have no difficulty recognising and accepting. In utopian fiction these conventions are reversed. It is the framework, not the story which is central, and the writer tries to achieve verisimilitude by using ordinary, everyday incidents to convey the peculiarities of her imaginary society. Utopian *theory* merely goes one step further and dispenses with the story altogether. But whether we are dealing with 'fiction' or 'theory', in either case the hallmark of utopian thought is this self-conscious rearrangement of the familiar social landscape. Utopians ask what the world would be like if features of social organisation which realists take for granted, were to be removed, replaced or reshaped.

This is not to say that the utopian imagination knows no bounds. For one thing, even hypothetical social formations must cohere. In general, if one or more structural elements in an interconnected system are altered, the consequences do not remain localised: the whole system is more or less radically transformed. And transformations, however dramatic or far-reaching, are not arbitrary—least of all in a procedure designed to exclude the unruliness of *real* historical change. Utopian thinkers are allowed to be vague or fanciful about the genesis (or whereabouts) of the ideal society: they are not expected to explain the transition from here (or now) to there (or then). But they must be more convincing when it comes to describing utopia itself, taking care to avoid resounding silences or jarring discords, and anticipating objections that would naturally occur to their readers. Above all, the different parts of utopia's social framework must fit comfortably together. One does not, for example, need to be a technological determinist to see the incongruity in William Morris's vision of a world which combines handicraft methods of production with an abundance of material goods.

But whilst even non-existent worlds must cohere, not all coherent worlds could exist. Tolkien's *Middle Earth*, for example, comes complete with its own language and lore, and although it is a world inhabited by wizards, hobbits and talking trees, it is neither chaotic nor arbitrary. Having distinguished between utopianism and realism, we need some way of demarcating both from fantasy.

Recall that utopia is not just a non-existent place: it is also somewhere good. Now, a make-believe world does not have to be excitingly better (or for that matter, alarmingly worse) than the real one. But the primary motivation for utopian speculation has been the belief that the human lot could, in some sense, be improved, at least in principle, if social arrangements were suitably refashioned. And we can only compare and evaluate alternative social arrangements, real or imaginary, if at least some aspects of the human condition are held constant. This is not just a matter of respecting the 'laws of physics': meaningful cross-cultural comparisons also presuppose some background uniformity in human biology and in the ways that human beings experience and respond to their conditions of life. If there were no transhistorical constancies in the human condition, we should find ourselves sealed inside a time capsule, unable to imagine that things had ever been or could ever be different. As Mary Midgley (1984: 106) puts it: 'If people were really natureless, were mere indefinite lumps of dough moulded entirely by historical forces, we could have no notion at all of what they would be like or how they would feel in any culture or epoch other than our own.'

As long as they steer clear of this relativist trap, utopias can be regarded as thought experiments in which certain features of the universe are held constant, including the nature of the human species, while social forms and cultural patterns are notionally varied and the results assessed according to some specified or implicit standard of evaluation. (There is, incidentally, no reason why utopia's moral community should not extend beyond human beings to include all the great apes, every kind of mammal or sentient life as a whole. The only limit is our capacity for empathy with species other than our own.) Actual speculative practice is, of course, a good deal less tidy than this. People argue endlessly about where to draw the line between nature and nurture and about what is to count as an improvement in the human (or animal) condition. And thought experiments are rarely dispassionate. There is a standing temptation to evade awkward questions and gloss over difficulties. And even free-thinking utopians have their blind spots. Until the twentieth century, for example, with the notable exception of Fourier, the majority of utopian writers showed no more awareness of gender than the most hidebound social realists. For all these reasons, beliefs about the limits of social possibility are contested and subject to revision. They tell us as much about those who hold them and the conditions in which they live as about the 'options' that would be open to us if, *per impossibile*, we could redesign society *ex novo*. Utopia is not to be found on any map. But the utopian tradition, like any other, has a history, with its own pattern of continuity and change. And the thought experiment remains an indispensable tool of applied social ethics. At root, utopians are tough-minded: they refuse to idealise either humanity or Nature and acknowledge the potential for conflict and disorder in all forms of human association. But they also refuse to allow social realists the last word about how to deal with these sempiternal problems, and insist on searching for better ways of handling both our metabolism with nature and our relations with each other. In a sense, as Davis (1981) points out, utopians idealise social organisation. But this comment is apt only on the understanding that 'organisation' is not synonymous with social engineering; and only if it is continually borne in mind that a thought experiment is neither a historical forecast nor a political manifesto.

The point of it all

In keeping with her expansive definition of utopia as a repository of desire, Levitas (op.cit.) stresses that utopian thought may serve a variety of purposes. As social criticism, it may express dissatisfaction with the status quo or offer a way of exploring and clarifying alternatives. Naturally, since both values and conjectures are matters of dispute, utopian criticism has a tendency to feed on itself. Thus, William Morris was moved to write *News From*

Nowhere in response to the prospect of regimented consumerism held out by Edward Bellamy (1982 [1888]). Similarly, in the twentieth century, Zamyatin, Huxley and Orwell all wrote dystopian critiques of state socialism. Utopias may also act as catalysts of social change, whether by galvanising discontent or by raising people's sights. And whatever their ideological and political impact, utopian visions may bring spiritual consolation, offering the soul a place of refuge and the heart a sense of hope.

In this essay I have accentuated the rationalist strand within utopian thought, emphasising its social character and dwelling in particular on the mainstream utopian tradition. Accordingly, without in any way denying that utopias are products of their time and place—quite the contrary—I want to stress their moral and intellectual significance. Consider the case of communism. I suggested earlier that communism could be interpreted as the limiting point on a spectrum of imaginary, but possible, social forms extending outwards (or 'forwards') from the existing social order. For the moment, just to fix ideas, I want to focus on the golden rule of distribution: 'From each according to his ability, to each according to his needs', abstracting from other aspects of the communist ideal. How can we make sense of this rule in a way that would enable us to compare a hypothetical communist society with the world as we know it?

For accounting purposes, the social product—what society finally gets from its recurrent economic efforts—can be divided into three categories: public goods, marketed commodities and private use-values. *Public goods* are enjoyed equally, at least in theory, by all members of society; are financed out of taxes; and are often, though by no means invariably, provided by the state. *Marketed commodities* may take the form of physical goods or 'invisible' services; may be produced by public or private enterprise; and may be purchased at the buyers' discretion, depending on their tastes and purchasing power. *Private use-values* are goods and services which people produce outside the cash nexus, either for themselves or for others, especially significant others. For comparative purposes, let us suppose that public expenditure and finance are divided into two separate branches: social transfers, which are financed entirely by an earmarked tax levied on personal earnings and property income; and public goods, which are financed from other sources of taxation. Social transfers may be distributed at various rates to various social units—individuals, families, households or other communal groups. They may also serve various purposes—to relieve or prevent poverty, to reduce social inequality, to preserve established hierarchies, to promote social cohesion, and so on—and eligibility rules will be framed accordingly, with entitlements based on need, work records or other indicators of merit.

Leaving aside the choice between alternative ways of paying for public goods, there are three dimensions in which social arrangements of this general kind could vary: adjustments could be made to the *composition of the social product*; to the proportion of society's monetised income which is devoted to social transfers or, for short, the *transfer ratio*; and to the *eligibility rules* governing who is entitled to how much by way of social transfers. Using this framework, we might say that as far as income distribution is concerned, a communist society would be one in which: (i) the composition of the social product is, in some sense, 'optimal'; (ii) the transfer ratio stands at 100 per cent; and (iii) all monetised income is distributed in the form of a universal grant, suitably graduated to take account of differential needs due to age and disability.

It would involve too much of a digression to discuss exactly what might be meant, in this context, by achieving an 'optimal balance between public goods, marketed commodities and private use-values'. Suffice it to say that none of these categories looks dispensable. One can easily imagine societies with no commodity production at all. One can also imagine societies where money will buy virtually anything. But it is hard to believe that either of these arrangements could ever be ideal. It is also worth noting that since the process of social reproduction tends to generate unwanted, and usually unintended, 'bads' as well as 'goods', a distributive regime based on the golden rule of communism would have to include not only a suitably comprehensive system of social accounting, but also a suitably democratic system for deciding the overall rate of economic growth and the general character of economic development.

This last point shows that communism, like any other social formation, must hang together. Beyond a certain point, it ceases to be useful to think about the distribution of income in isolation from the division of labour and the distribution of power. This does not, however, mean that there is no point in conceptually taking the social framework apart. Apart from the fact that it is impossible to deal with everything at once, dealing methodically with one thing at a time helps to make it clear that utopias are hypotheses and nothing more. Neither pure communism nor unadulterated capitalism marks the 'end of history'. What could this phrase possibly mean as long as the human race is still around? Rather, such ideal forms are limiting cases. With respect to the distribution of income, the opposite of pure communism would be a veritable paradise of possessive individualism in which people have no social rights and obligations whatsoever: there are no public goods (or taxes to pay for them); the transfer ratio is zero; and those in need must look to charity, theft or extortion. (One might, of course, wonder whether social order is possible at all without some element of public reciprocity. But that is precisely the point). Strung out between these two extremes is a range of intermediate worlds, including the status quo, which happens to be the one that currently occupies social space.

There is, then, no need to choose between analysis and synthesis: we can and should use both. Having identified whatever we take to be the main dimensions of the social framework, we can either explore each one in turn, or try to form a composite image of utopia as a whole. 'Fiction' is the natural medium for depicting the good society in the round; the more analytical methods of utopian theory are better suited to examining its social anatomy. But in any case, it is less important to worry about how utopian thought is expressed, than to keep on expressing it.

Why? Why is it important to insist that the society in which we live is merely one of many possible forms of social life, some of them mere theoretical limits, even when we strongly suspect that the best of all possible worlds is destined to remain forever beyond our reach? There are, I think, three reasons. One stems from the distinction, mentioned earlier, between what would be best in the abstract and what is best all things considered. In both personal life and politics we are frequently obliged to weigh moral claims—claims about what is good, right or just—against considerations such as everyday reasonableness, cost-effectiveness, harmful side effects and irreducible uncertainty. But it is simply impossible to do this unless we maintain a distinction between ideals and realities.

Suppose we are confronted by some evil, wrong or injustice which we are powerless to resist. Rather than indulge in heroic, but futile gestures, it may be wiser to bide our time, accepting, for the moment, that the balance of forces is against us. This is bad enough. It is even worse to be pressured into declaring that might is right, and worst of all if one starts to believe it. To guard against moral degradation, we need at least to clarify the conflicting demands of morality and expediency. And to do this we need the intellectual freedom to step back from the flux of events and suspend judgement about even the most deep-rooted and long-lasting of out social arrangements. Utopia gives us this freedom.

A second reason for seeking to perpetuate the utopian tradition is that what people believe about the way their society works and the limits of social possibility, is itself one of the factors that determines the course of events. If most people are convinced that the way things are is the way they *must* be, not just in the short run, but in the long run too, then the existing order is that much more secure. By contrast, when people begin to think the unthinkable, the situation becomes more fluid. Hence, even though utopia is not to be found on any map, thinking about it can still help to change the world.

The final reason for cherishing the capacity to imagine wholesale alternatives to the established social order is that ethics without sociology is empty. It is not enough to enunciate abstract principles of liberty, democracy or justice: we need to know what difference it would make if society could somehow be remade in their image. (Anyone who answers: 'None', is presumably inviting us to believe that the world is already ideal.) This is because it is usually hard to know what a principle means until we spell out exactly how we think it should be enacted. Take the case of universal suffrage. If this is construed as requiring not just 'one adult, one vote', but also 'one vote, one value', it is by no means obvious which of the various possible voting systems is the best way to secure it. Moreover, the merits of different systems are likely to vary in different contexts.

Ethics and vision

An even more apposite example of the essentially complementary relationship between ethical reasoning and utopian speculation is the concept of justice as fairness proposed by Rawls (1972). A system of arrangements is fair, Rawls suggests, if people could agree to it without knowing whether it will benefit them personally. To develop this idea, he conducts the following thought experiment. Imagine that the citizens of some well-ordered state are transported into what Rawls calls the 'original position'. Here they undergo the sociological equivalent of sensory deprivation: each person's knowledge of his or her current and prospective social identity, values, position and interests is obliterated. At a stroke, the established social order is deconstructed and people are invited to think about how to put it back together again.

Rawls assumes that his experimental subjects possess no more than average human intelligence, capacity for empathy with others, understanding of human nature and knowledge of social institutions. He also assumes that they retain the formal status of citizenship, though exactly what this status entails is for them to decide. To this end, they are presented with a shortlist of general principles reflecting all the various comprehensive ethical and religious outlooks which have gained a following in their society. From this list they are required to choose the one(s) which they wish to see embodied in their future social arrangements, knowing that they will have to live with the consequences, but without knowing what the consequences will be for them personally. People may take as long as they like to reach what Rawls calls 'reflective equilibrium', shifting back and forth between possible worlds and the original position, in order to work through the consequences of alternative regimes.

If people were obliged to act as moral legislators in this way, they would first have to decide on the 'currency' of distributive justice: what, in other words, are the social advantages or assets whose distribution is somehow to be regulated. Rawls comes down in favour of what he calls primary goods, which he divides into four categories: rights and liberties; opportunities and powers; income and wealth; and the social bases of self-respect. In *A Theory of Justice*, he justifies this choice on the grounds that primary goods are prerequisites for any conception of the good life. But this is an empirical claim which could conceivably be falsified. Someone might, for example, want to live as a slave. To avoid this objection, in his later work, Rawls shifts his ground to the ethical claim that primary goods are preconditions for the exercise of autonomous moral choice (Rawls, 1980).

The legislators' next problem is to decide the basic rules which are to govern the distribution of primary goods and which must, somehow, be built into their social order. From the shortlist before them, they settle on three. The first, which takes precedence over the other two, is the principle of *maximum equal liberty*. This accords each person an equal right to the most extensive scheme of liberties compatible with the same liberties for everyone else. The second, which takes precedence over the third, is the principle of *fair equality of opportunity*. Rawls interprets this to mean that it should be equally possible for all equally talented persons to attain any given office or social position. The third is the well known, if somewhat inaptly named, *difference principle*. This requires that the remaining primary goods be distributed in such a way as to leave the least advantaged class of persons at least as well-off as the class that would be least advantaged under any other arrangement. This criterion is sometimes referred to as the 'maximin' rule because it ranks alternatives by the worst outcome.

There are many well known objections to the Rawlsian enterprise, but my concern here is simply to establish what kind of enterprise it is. The fiction of the original position suggests that Rawls's theory might be assimilated to the utopian tradition. Yet Rawls refrains from spelling out its implications for the design of social institutions. Having formulated the principles of justice, he stops short of telling us how they could or should be implemented and sustained. In this sense, his work does not quite qualify as utopian theory, still less as utopian fiction. We might describe it as an invitation or prelude to utopian speculation. This is, of course, exactly what we would expect from a theory which seeks to remain neutral as between rival conceptions of the good life. It does, however, imply that the principles of justice can accommodate more than one interpretation.

Consider, for example, the difference principle. This serves as a criterion for deciding on fair inequalities in the distribution of income, wealth and the social bases of self-respect. It is clearly intended to bring individual rights, social inequalities and economic performance into a common framework. If it can be shown that some structural inequality serves either to raise the total output of social goods produced at a given cost, or to reduce the cost of producing a given output, then as long as the inequality in question satisfies the maximin test, it counts as fair.

Suppose, for the sake of argument, that everyone accepts the difference principle as the appropriate criterion for arranging social inequalities—in preference, say, to the utilitarian greatest happiness principle or a commitment to possessive individualism. Even so, people may still take different views about the appropriate definition of the relevant primary goods. As we saw earlier, in any distributive scheme there are choices to be made about the composition of the social product. Likewise, what counts as an asset is equally open to different interpretations. Society's wealth may be broadly defined to include environmental endowments, social institutions, moral and intellectual traditions, civic virtues and human knowledge, or it may be restricted to natural resources, capital equipment and technological prowess. And a whole variety of conditions may affect a person's self-esteem, ranging from emotional security in childhood and ongoing intimacy with others to participation in socially valued activities. Given that there is no single 'currency' of distributive justice, disputes about the proper scope of the maximin rule are bound to lead to disagreement about the design of the just society. One can, of course, evade the issue by leaving the specification of 'primary goods' open-ended. In effect, this is what Rawls does. But then the difference principle becomes an algebraic formula with a range of possible values.

Moreover, even if people were agreed about *what* is to be *maximised*, there would still be room for dispute about just *how much* inequality should be sanctioned. Suppose everyone accepts some measure of per capita income as the appropriate indicator of economic performance and wishes to discover whether existing inequalities in income are justified in the sense that the lowest incomes are at least as high as they would be under any alternative arrangement. The answer will depend, among other things, on what economic incentives are necessary to induce people to contribute their time, energies, skills and other resources to the process of social production. But what people need by way of incentives is not determined entirely by human nature: it varies from one culture to another. Thus anyone who subscribes to Rawls's theory, wants to know what a just society would look like, and is genuinely prepared to consider any form of social life that is humanly possible, had better be prepared for some serious utopian study.

References

Beecher, J., *Charles Fourier—The visionary and his world* (Berkeley, California, 1986).
Bellamy, E., *Looking Backward From the Year 2000* (Harmondsworth, 1982 [1888]).
Davis, J.C., *Utopia and the Ideal Society* (Cambridge, 1981).
Engels, F., *Socialism Utopian and Scientific* in 'Marx-Engels Selected Works' (London, 1970 [1892]).
James, W., 'The Dilemma of Determinism' in *The Will to Power and Other Essays in Popular Philosophy* (New York, 1897).
Kumar, K., *Utopianism* (Milton Keynes, 1991).
Levitas, R., *The Concept of Utopia* (London, 1990).
Manuel, F. E. and Manuel, F. P., *Utopian Thought in the Western World* (Oxford, 1979).
Midgley, M., *Wickedness: A Philosophical Essay* (London, 1984).
More, Thomas, *Utopia* (Harmondsworth, 1965 [1516]).
Morris, W., *News From Nowhere* (London, 1970 [1891]).
Nozick, R., *Anarchy, State and Utopia* (Oxford, 1974).
Rawls, R., *A Theory of Justice* (Oxford, 1972).
Rawls, J., 'Kantian Construction in Moral Theory', *Journal of Philosophy* 77 (1980).
Thoreau, H., 'Walden' in *The Portable Thoreau* (Harmondsworth, 1977 [1854]).

'Utopia' in British Political Culture
The desire that dare not speak its name

Philip Coupland

C.B. Purdom's declaration in the face of a world of poverty, tyranny and war was that 'Utopia has to be established to save us from destruction'. Gerald Abrahams, surveying the means available to the modern state, saw 'the world' equipped with 'a large part of the technical equipment that is required in order to run a Utopia'.[1] However, while the bulk of socialist and 'progressive' opinion during the 1930s and the war years shared Purdom's conviction of the pressing need to transcend the social order of liberal capitalism and Abraham's faith in the means to do so, their embrace of utopianism was seldom so open, free and unembarrassed. Utopia was more often the desire that dare not speak its name.

The intention of this article is to examine the utterances of, first, what might be collectively called the parties of British democratic socialism of the 1930s and 1940s—Labour, the Independent Labour Party and Common Wealth—and, second, the Communist Party of Great Britain for indications from their uses of the term 'utopia' of its meaning and place in the culture and praxis of the politics of the time.[2] While the meaning of 'utopia' (and thus 'utopianism') as a concept has been a matter of considerable debate, it is operationally defined here as signifying the human desire for, and the conscious effort to imagine a better life, as expressed in more or less detailed proposals towards, 'blueprints' for, and descriptions of, ways of life and social institutions not yet in existence.[3] In addition, this article is informed by the belief that the use of the concept of utopia is a valid and fruitful tool in historical analysis and that utopia as a 'repository of desire' and a space for the critical imagination to freely utilise, is also of present and enduring value.[4]

'Utopia' was born in the act of criticising the status quo and could only exist as an alternative posited, in relation, and reaction to, an existing social order. Those whose interests lay in maintaining the belief that life could be no different, naturally condemned all alternatives which challenged it as fanciful, impossible or at least impractical, in short 'utopian' and, in the period in question, this meaning was reflected by the standard definition of the term. This was, as Lucian Hölscher has shown, a meaning which became embedded in the language by its currency in polemics at moments of social and political upheaval in the centuries following More. Similarly, during the inter-war period Laski could write ironically 'no effort is more suspect in our time than the criticism of the existing rights of property. It is wrong because it is subversive. It is futile because it is Utopian. It is erroneous because it runs counter to the eternal laws of human nature.'[5] The convenient conflation of the absolutely impossible with that which was merely incompatible with the existing social order was apparent when a local debating society imagined itself as the 'Government of Utopia' and called for both 'a maximum of 30 hours per week for factory workers' and for 'Skyhooks and wire netting' to be used to prevent hail storms. When linked to the British tradition of anti-intellectualism and brute empiricism, this anti-utopianism was given an added charge and, in this vein, Harold Macmillan distanced himself from 'the dreamer of Utopias' with their 'mystical conceptions of the future of society' 'foreign to the practical mind of the ordinary adult British citizen'.[6]

The inverse of [e]utopia—the good society—is of course dystopia, a term whose first recorded use was in the eighteenth century.[7] However, because utopia already signified the 'good' society which, because it ran against the laws of nature, was inevitably bad in practice, dystopia was a superfluous, and seldom used term, as its place in the chain of signification was already taken. The quotation of Nicolas Berdyaev's words that 'Les utopies sont réalisables' by Aldous Huxley as the epigraph for his highly influential Brave New World—operated within this discourse of utopia as dystopia.[8] Furthermore, three of the most well known anti-socialist polemics of the period by W. H. Chamberlin, Eugene Lyons—both appropriately enough choices of the Right Book Club—and F.A. Hayek ironically cast socialism in general, and the Soviet Union in particular, as 'utopias', so dismissing them and utopianism generally as anything but roads to the good society.[9]

The intention behind the debasement of utopia into a political insult was to deny the possibility of change and freeze the institutions of society in a perpetual present. As Stafford Cripps pointed out, the 'argument' that socialism was 'Utopian' was 'the stock in trade of those who resist change and who fear its consequences to themselves. Every advance that has been made by civilisation has been announced as ridiculous and Utopian at some time in our history. The idea of flight was ridiculed until men flew.' Similarly R.W.G. Mackay saw that 'there was no reform of any substantial nature, at any time in the world, which has not been dismissed as visionary or Utopian.'[10]

It was as if by breaking the link between the signifier and the signified that the concept of an alternative future, and so its function, could be eliminated from political culture. Without the nowhere of imagination, desire and social critique would have no space into which they might be projected. Without the vision of an alternative future, there would be no point of reference or motivating goal for political praxis. However, the will-to-utopia never rested in its attempts to subvert this repression in language and find expression in thought and practice. The circumstances of the time made the need for utopia pressing. Symbolic of this, the *New Statesman and Nation* recorded in late 1931 that 'the old comparatively stable world seems suddenly to have collapsed' and that measures which could 'no longer be treated as the fantasies of Utopia-mongers' were 'demanded by common sense.'[11]

Apart from being used in a bid to denigrate, and so neutralise challenges to the status quo, utopia suffered another blow to its legitimacy by fulfilling a similar function in exchanges between competing challengers to the established order. Each party claimed the sole title to truth and hence that only its prescription could create a better world. Clement Attlee sounded much like Macmillan when declaring that Labour was set apart by its 'characteristic practicality' from the 'theorists or revolutionaries who were so absorbed in Utopian dreams that they were unwilling to deal with the actualities of everyday life'. Returning the favour, the *Daily Worker* declared that Britain Without Capitalists would make clear that the 'solutions' of '"The Next Five Years," of the Labour Party with its "public corporations", are Utopian' while the Communists' depiction 'of a new and glorious Britain and the creation of an entirely new type of man' was declared elsewhere to be 'not a Utopian enquiry but a practical survey'.[12]

The language of democratic socialists fully demonstrated the ambivalence contingent in the coexistence of both the debased concept of utopia and the fact that without the true substance of utopia as a transcendent goal, the whole existence of these parties was pointless. G.D.H. Cole suggested that the Labour Movement was 'Utopian, in that it has made its appeal by presenting a vision of the superior merits of a socialist society.' A reading of Paul Bloomfield's history of utopian writing prompted another Labour socialist to comment that 'the making of Utopia is man's attempt to recreate his present life to suit his own human purpose. Utopia is a vision of his work accomplished' and that 'every Socialist has his pet Utopia'. The town of Kettering, while bearing 'no resemblance to the rectangular townships of which Robert Owen dreamed', was nonetheless 'On the Road to Utopia' due to the efforts of the local Co-operative society. Nancy Adam's suggestion was that electricity would allow the 'modern housewife' to 'switch to utopia'. Councillor James Bugby of Northampton described 'Utopia' for Primrose Hill Men's Fireside: 'No rents, rates or taxes', 'No unemployment', 'No more war', 'A three hour working day', 'Great national medical services', 'Wider streets', 'Electric buses', 'No need for money'.[13]

Laski admitted, with Wilde, that 'it is a poor map on which one's eye does not see Utopia'.[14] But at the same time, as the comment of Attlee quoted above suggests, Labour always sought to locate itself in a tradition of socialism which was definitively British; one centred on practice rather than guided by theory, empirical not abstract, orientated towards 'practical' aims tomorrow rather than 'pie in the sky' in the far-off future. In this vein Dalton distanced himself from utopianism with faint praise, commenting that while 'an elaborate theoretical study of an ideal society' was 'stimulating', it was a 'different kind of exercise' from 'practical politics'. It was 'better to decide the direction of advance than to debate the details of Utopia'. Durbin stressed the urgency of basic reforms because just as 'a starving man cannot fully enjoy the beauty of the stars' so a 'depressed society cannot concern itself primarily with an egalitarian Utopia'. Strachey sought to impress on his reader 'Socialism is not Utopia. The establishment of a socialist society does not suddenly make people into saints and heroes'.[15]

In many cases such statements reflected the underlying conflict between the aim of socialism and the ideals of gradualism and 'practicality'. Common Wealth's proposals for common ownership and the revolution in behaviour implied by its goal of 'Vital Democracy' were among the more radical of the programmes pursued during wartime. In consequence the Party was especially urgent in its denials of utopianism. CW listed among the 'pitfalls for the unwary':

> Utopianism. Whatever the angle of approach we should never infer that it is possible to make the world perfect overnight. We should never allow people to suppose that CW is some sort of clever trick which is going to produce for them an easy Paradise dropping automatically into their laps. If people mean to work together scientifically and diligently in democratic politics we can be optimistic without being oversanguine that we can expect a substantial advance towards human brotherhood; we cannot expect miracles.

For all these denials it was clear that Common Wealth practice and policy were deeply utopian, putting forward a radical alternative to liberal capitalism, which Richard Acland, the party's founder, laid out in detail in *What It Will Be Like In the New Britain*. Acland's warning not to 'expect Utopia in 1950, or even 1975' with its sub-text of the possibility of utopia, is an eloquent expression of the coexistence of the will to utopia and the imperatives of anti-utopia.[16]

As the quotation from the *New Statesman and Nation* above suggests, it was at moments of greatest need when the dominant meaning of utopia was most obviously contested at the heart of the political process. Concluding his wartime blueprint for the socialist Britain, Aneurin Bevan admitted it might appear to be 'a highly artificial conception', 'made entirely in the abstract' and thus 'one of those Utopias which we can sit down and easily draft'. But the demands of the time legitimated utopia: 'the framework of the past had been broken, and a new frame had to be.' The often heard admission that a proposal 'sounded extremely Utopian' but was nevertheless 'the only real hope for the world' was the expression of the will-to-utopia rejecting its repression.[17]

Utopia was functional not only in moments of crisis but central to the whole human striving to transcend the limitations of the present, to expand continually the envelope of the possible. Barbara Wootton's articulation of Labour's rejection of other forms of socialism made full use of the anti-utopian discourse, dismissing the 'change-the-system attitude' which rejected partial reform as 'an example of the dangerous variety of utopianism' and 'pure fantasy'. However, Wootton then went on to make clear that the 'utopianism' of 'revolutionaries' was not the only one. The 'label "utopian"' was 'not necessarily pejorative'. She continued:

> There are in fact two forms of utopianism....The admirable and useful form is the utopianism of those who advocate policies which appear to the promoters to be themselves desirable, but unattainable so long as other people do not share their opinion....But the fact that other people do not already agree with an opinion is the silliest reason for keeping quiet about it. If your view is right, how can others accept it, if they are not to hear of it? If it is wrong, how can you see what is wrong with it, if they never have a chance to tell you....It is the plain lesson of experience that desirable reforms begin as paradoxes and end as common places.... If the charge of utopianism is used to inhibit the expression of opinions that are still at the ridiculous stage, they will all, sensible and silly alike, remain permanently at that stage.

In like vein Leonard Woolf believed that 'the term utopia is commonly used in two different ways'. The first usage being when 'we speak of a dream or a policy being utopian in the sense that it contains a purpose or is based on a hope or ideal which is incapable of fulfilment'; the second usage 'in the sense of "unreal" as opposed to "reality"' because it aims at an unattained ideal or objective. Woolf recognised that 'all policies, even of the most realist statesmen aim at unattained ideals or objectives'.[18]

The unexplored implication of Wootton and Woolf's distinction between the two forms of utopianism was that the difference between the 'admirable', 'useful' and 'real' utopianism and the 'unreal', 'dangerous' and 'fantas[tic]' utopianism was inherently subjective. Seldom, if ever, did utopianism employ the 'sky-hooks' mentioned above and so be beyond the belief of all but the insane. There could be no meaningful absolute distinction of the type suggested by Wootton and Woolf, utopia could only exist as a space of democratic and equal access. Utopianism, while being no closer to holding a legitimate place in the political lexicon was, as Wootton and Woolf's words made clear, functionally essential, whatever name it might be given.

If the function of utopianism was central to the possibility of creating visions of an alternative future, in a parliamentary democracy it was also vital to the efforts of a party to recruit support via what can be called the 'education of desire'. I.O. Evans, himself an author of a children's book imagining a technologically sophisticated future, believed that '"Utopianisations" may be of service, for after all, before we are ready to make our minds up to work for anything we must first convince ourselves that it is worth having when we have reached it. So we may be spurred to work to bring about the Co-operative Commonwealth.' Somewhat more grudgingly a reviewer of S.G. Hobson's *Functional Socialism* admitted that although the author's 'whole method' was 'Utopian' that 'there may be some value in that—for some sorts of public' because 'intelligent middle-class folk like to look before they leap'.[19]

The reviewer of Hobson's work added the rider that 'the trouble is that no one really knows what is going to follow the Social Revolution' which begged the question of quite why anyone would wish to sacrifice anything for the unknown. In contrast, Cripps, in his introduction to Gilbert Mitchison's *The First Workers' Government*, was more ready to allow for a legitimate function of utopianism, noting that 'the long-anticipated journey of the workers out of capitalism into a new and better economic system, has led to a great deal of speculation in the past. Utopias of all kinds have been pictured. We have delighted to discuss the journey and speculate upon the sort of country that we may reach.' However, once again, the ambivalent meaning of utopia made its presence known as Cripps distinguished

Mitchison's imaginative history of a socialist government written in 1980 from the 'utopian' by the impossible claims that it was a 'history of the future, and the sketching of the actual progress of the building'.[20]

Ethel Mannin despaired that in wartime Britain it seemed that 'Utopia is to be translated into terms of the Beveridge Report and Mr. Churchill's uninspired programme' and offered instead *Bread and Roses: An Utopian Survey and Blue Print*.[21] Although this was the only such text to call itself utopian, there was no lack of what were utopian blueprints and 'word pictures' by any other name.

In addition to Acland's vision of the 'New Britain', Emmanuel Shinwell described what he would like to see in the post war period. Some years earlier George Lansbury had evoked the vision of the England he desired and ILP leader James Maxton wrote of the 'new world' which he would create if he were made dictator.[22] Attlee, while making clear that he was 'not going to try to picture a Utopia', in sketching the 'Co-operative Commonwealth' inevitably had to imagine elements of a society which did not yet exist and whose 'practicality' rested on arguments and assumptions which were necessarily subjective and contestable. Sketching out Labour's plans for new homes, Attlee commented that 'all this may sound utopian, but if we realise that there are men out of work, and being paid by the State for doing nothing, it begins to sound more reasonable.' In a particularly vivid example, Mercer claimed that 'the creation of a Co-operative Commonwealth is no longer a utopian dream' and could see 'the sunlit towers and minarets of the Co-operative Commonwealth of Great Britain clearly visible of the horizon of Time'.[23] These are examples of the more obvious manifestations of democratic socialist utopianism but even the most mundane pamphlet, inasmuch as it was orientated towards objects which were not yet in existence, employed the function of utopia. As Labour contended in relation to its proposals for the Empire: 'there may be those who think that such a policy and programme is unwise or Utopian. The Labour Party believes it to be wise and practicable.'[24]

Cripps at Labour's 1945 party conference stressed that they 'should not lead people to believe it was some easy Utopia into which they were invited to stay' but that year also wrote of the possibility of realising 'the Utopia which, in one form or another, has been so often pictured for us as the ideal at which we aim'.[25] This last, straightforward use of the term to describe the object which Labour socialist praxis strove towards was a move beyond the protocols of the language of 'practical' socialism. Instead, in 1945 Labour's utopia was called 'a better Britain...'; 'a better' or 'a happier future'; 'better and happier days'; a 'better world'; 'a Socialist Commonwealth of

Great Britain'; 'a New Britain', 'a NEW BRITAIN where unemployment and poverty shall be abolished'; a 'New and Better Britain'; 'a new age of peace and abundance'; 'a brighter "New World"'; 'a brighter and better world'; a 'new world of Hope, Promise and Achievement'; 'a New Social Order'; 'a new world'; 'a new order of society, giving to our people a fuller and better life'; a "Golden age" and even, in Weston-Super-Mare, 'a new way of life'.[26]

Ironically, the synonym for dystopia introduced into the language by Aldous Huxley was, on occasion, preferred as the name of the object of desire. Two years after the publication of *Brave New World* the editor of the *New Clarion* could write, without irony, of himself and his colleagues as 'the strange people who are to make the brave new world' and Leah L'Estrange Malone, writing in wartime under the heading 'Forward to a Brave New World' declared that 'when victory is won we must build our brave new world.'[27]

At one level Karl Mannheim's *Ideology and Utopia* (1936)[28] might have been seen as a basis for utopia to become more than, as a reviewer suggested, a 'mere delusion'. Mannheim clearly spelled out that it was 'always the dominant group which determined what is to be regarded as utopian' and not because such ideas were absolutely unrealisable, but because they could only come by 'shattering, either partially or wholly, the order of things prevailing at the time.' The 'road of history', Mannheim wrote, 'leads from one topia over a utopia to the next topia'.

However, not only was Mannheim's work, in the opinion of A.L. Rowse 'almost impossible to read' but even for those who persevered, it was ambiguous in its message. In particular, we might note that Mannheim laid a particular duty on intellectuals to meet the 'need for an imperative (a utopia) to drive us onward'. The alternative being 'the disappearance of utopia' and 'a static state of affairs in which man himself becomes no more than a thing'. However, at the same time, while Mannheim argued for the 'necessity of wilfully choosing our course' his argument was that utopia was something only discernible with hindsight which 'every age allows to arise'. This reading was detectable in Laski's understanding of the moment of transformation as one when 'ideologies and Utopias are compelled to adapt themselves to a changing environment'.[29] For Mannheim the nature of utopia preceded individual consciousness, contemplation, and imagination and was thus a space which was already full and so closed to use. Perhaps reflecting this, Mannheim's thesis' most significant impact in British political writing was in the mangled and opportunistic use of it by E.H. Carr.[30]

A similar way of avoiding the taint of 'utopianism' was the Fabian argument that a socialist society was not 'utopian' because it emerged via the 'process' of history.[31] Fred Henderson allowed that 'when anyone begins to talk to you about the goal of a movement you have a natural suspicion that he is about to recite his dreams to you; visions of Utopia unrelated to the real facts and the limitations of life; something that may be a heart's desire, but inaccessible except in such dreams'. In contrast to this hypothetical dreamer, Henderson pledged that 'in speaking of the goal of Socialism' he would lay out 'an interpretation of the movement of history; of the discernible purpose towards which the forces now visibly operating in the world's life are carrying our civilisation'. However, wishing to seize the discourse of scientific certainty without denying utopian desire, Henderson argued that while it was 'the existing and known facts that preach our Socialist gospel' it was also 'true enough' that the 'new social order' would be 'the fulfilment of dreams and of the heart's desires of men' albeit 'dreams and desires of things discerned as possible and on offer in the world of facts'.[32] All other versions of the good society presumably being based on things discerned as impossible and on the world of fiction.

Communist Party perspectives

Turning from democratic socialism to the Communist Party, 'utopian meaning something idealistic and unrealisable', was a favourite term of abuse against those outside of the party, like Strachey in 1940, or 'slander' when attached to Morris when he was appropriated as a Communist hero. The notion of the form of the good society as something beyond human will and imagination—not the invention of dreamers (Utopians), but the 'inevitable outcome of modern capitalist society'—also reached its dogmatic height.[33] Utopianism was prohibited despite, as Berki has explained, the future communist society being the only thing that made Marxist thought logical and Communist praxis comprehensible. Furthermore, this prohibition ignored the fact that Marx's 'vision' of communist society preceded his historical and sociological 'insight' as the point of reference for his critique of capitalism. However, the claim of Marxism to an epistemological status akin to the natural sciences precluded imaginative speculation about that which was not yet: communism. So, communism while 'the innermost essence or hub of Marx's thought' at the same time 'either had no content', or a content 'beyond words'.[34] The consequence of this prohibition on imagining the future was the deeply entrenched antinomy between 'Science' (good) and 'Utopianism' (bad) established by the classic works of Marx and Engels which, as E.P. Thompson suggests, meant that 'at any point after 1850 Scientific Socialism had no more need for Utopias (and doctrinal authority for suspecting them). Speculation as to the society of the future was repressed, and displaced by attention to strategy.'[35]

However, if the vision of communist society was central to communism as a movement, and utopia is an archetypal vehicle of desire in Western culture then we should expect that utopianism, like the Freudian Eros, would seek a path through repression to find expression. Thus, while excised in name from Communist language, at the same time the practices of utopianism suffused the culture of the party. An invitation in the *Daily Worker* to 'meet the utopians!' at a dance at St George's Town Hall, Cable Street was more revelatory than ironic.[36]

One path through repression was via word games. The reviewer of John Langdon-Davies' *A Short History of the Future* signalled his entry into a controversial area, commenting that the book's 'prophecies concerning the future Communist Society, although belonging to the realm of speculation, will prove most popular'. Elsewhere the same volume was exonerated from 'utopianism' as 'prophecy inspired not by vain wish dreams but by direct contact with the stage of action.'[37] Allen Hutt, reviewing Bernal's *The Social Function of Science*, noted that its author wrote of 'what might be'. Perhaps sensing that he was straying into forbidden territory Hutt wrote that Benal 'while repudiating Utopian speculation, indicates some of the ways in which science could already be employed to transform the life of man and the satisfaction of his needs'. Could 'Utopian' and 'scientific' speculation be so divided and, if so, how? Bernal considered his 'forecast' to be 'in no sense Utopian' because it 'does not suggest any changes which we cannot see a way to realize'. But utopians like Wells, let alone everyone that the CPGB labelled as utopian, seldom consciously introduced the impossible into their blueprints for the future.[38]

Undoubtedly the major path through repression for the CPGB, as it was to a lesser extent with other parties,[39] was via the projection of its utopian desire onto a space which, unlike the nowhere of utopian imagination was in the concrete terrestrial present and so a legitimate repository of desire. Strachey wrote of the circumstances of this innovation:

> Marx derived the basic principles of socialism. from his critique of capitalism. But he would have forfeited his right to be called a scientist, and become a mere spinner of fancies, if he had claimed to be able to describe the society of the future in any greater detail than this. And if we are now able to fill in a certain amount of that detail, that is only because a socialist society is now arising in the Soviet Union.

In 1917, 'four centuries and one year after the publication of Thomas More's book' Strachey wrote, the dream and the circumstances for its realisation came together when the 'germ' of socialism 'in More's *Utopia*' came 'to its full maturity in the theory and practice of Lenin'. Strachey noted the 'remarkable passages in the *Utopia*' which anticipated 'practices which are actually developing in the Soviet Union to-day.'[40]

By this circuitous path the utopian imagination could escape from its suppression to embody its longing in words. After 1917 the central narrative of Communist utopianism was, as the *Daily Worker* put it, that the 'Soviet Union Shows the Way to a Worker's Britain'.[41] Seemingly constructed from real matter, photos, statistics, government reports and so on, rather than airy imaginings, imagination constructed a communist utopia called the USSR which could then be spoken of without being doctrinally 'utopian'. For the interested Briton, able and willing to believe, the Soviet Union could be 'a dream come true'. Apart from visions forged on the spot of a 'new life so happy and splendid', Britain had its own body of writing constructing the USSR as utopia—the 'new civilisation' of the Webbs, Pat Sloan's Russia where 'democracy' was made 'ever more real', Hewlett Johnson's vision of the 'Socialist Sixth of the World': 'not a Utopian world' but nonetheless one imbued with the possibility of 'a nobler and more enduring goodness and beauty'. The USSR was the 'Land Where Dreams Come True' and the CPGB's programme for much of the period declared its aim as being 'For Soviet Britain'.[42]

At the moment of the apparent vindication of the legitimacy of the utopian imagination, its place in communist political culture had been imperiously seized—the Utopian Socialism of Thomas More and Robert Owen became the Scientific Socialism of our day'. With the validity of utopianism firmly located in the past, the imagination of British communists was cribbed and confined on the procrustean bed of Stalinism, just as the actuality of utopian experimentation was crushed in the USSR. Orwell indicted the then current 'nexus of thought, "Socialism-progress-machinery-Russia-tractors-hygiene-machinery-progress" as anything but an educator of desire'.[43]

J. Allen Skinner's view of socialist thought in the 1940s found it 'overgrown by the jungle tangle of "dialectics"' and he issued 'A plea for Utopianism'. Socialism, Skinner argued, had not only lost contact with 'an avowed body of moral conceptions, of ideas as to what is good' but also suffered 'from the absence of the means of intellectually projecting these moral conceptions, these ideas of the good, on to the social field by means of methods of thought that it has become the fashion to decry as "Utopianism"'. The function and value of utopianism was, Skinner averred, as a means 'to translate individual morality into social plans for the good life', and while it was the case that in doing so the means to those ends might be insufficiently considered, the 'present defect' was the 'obsession with means to the exclusion of ends'. What was required was 'the rehabilitation of "Utopianism"' as 'a means of bringing back the badly needed conception of the factor of will into socialist politics'. Skinner's argument was not with 'Marxism as a philosophy and certainly not of Marxism as a system of economic analysis' but with the tendency to employ Marxism without a positive concept of the end desired, having 'no other criterion of the desirable than the actual trend that things are taking'.[44]

Utopia silenced?

Although I have drawn only on texts of the period before 1945, it is not unreasonable to offer a few tentative comments on the place of utopia in political culture in the twentieth century more generally. Indeed, after 1945 the visions and agendas of, on one hand, democratic socialism and, on the other, state socialism were dominant ideological forces until the rise of the New Right, the hegemony of free market economics, and the fall of 'communism'.

In response to these last developments, that section of opinion which had ironically labelled the dystopian state-socialist societies 'utopia' as a prophylactic, could proclaim these developments as marking the 'end of history' and, consequently, the 'death' of utopia.[45] In this respect, Marxism-Leninism's dogmatic and vocal proclamation of itself as the sole heir of the utopian tradition was a gift to those who also—albeit for different reasons—were eager to see the utopian voice silenced. However, on the eve of the millennium, the British democratic socialist tradition is seemingly no more friendly to the utopian imagination, offering little more than a rigid belief in market economics and the empty signifier of a 'new Britain' as its 'utopia'. In 1999 we might agree with Skinner's conclusion half a century ago that 'unless the human will counts for something democracy is clearly a meaningless conception; and it may be Utopian, but it is far from impractical, to hold the view that if the human will counts it must sometimes be directed against, rather than with the mere mechanical tendency of things.'[46]

Notes

My thanks go to James Hinton for reading and commenting on this article. All errors, omissions and conclusions are of course my own.

1. C.B. Purdom, *The New Order* (London, 1941), p.5; Gerald Abrahams. *The World Turns Left* (London, 1943), p.8. Except for references to the work of Thomas More and uses in quotations, 'utopia' as a generic term is not capitalised.
2. For a general history of the usage of the term 'utopia', see the important article by Lucian Hölscher: 'Utopie', *Utopian Studies*, Vol.7, No.9, 1996. pp.1–65.
3. See J.C. Davis, 'The History of Utopia: the Chronology of Nowhere', in Peter Alexander and Roger Gill (eds), *Utopias* (London, 1984), pp.1–17; Ruth Levitas, *The Concept of Utopia*, Hemel Hempstead, 1990, passim; Lucy Sargisson *Contemporary Feminist Utopianism* (London, 1996), Part 1.
4. For utopia as a 'repository of desire' see Levitas, op. cit. The investigation of the utopian qualities of politics and culture in the late modern period in the sense understood here is at a relatively early stage, examples include: Richard Stites, *Revolutionary Dreams: Utopian Vision and Experimental Life in the Russian Revolution* (New York, 1989); Patrick Joyce, *Visions of the People: Industrial England and the Question of Class, 1848–1914* (Cambridge, 1991); Helmut Gruber, *Red Vienna: Experiment in Working-Class Culture 1919–1934* (New York, 1991); Peter Beilharz, *Labour's Utopias: Bolshevism, Fabianism, Social Democracy* (London, 1993); Roger Griffin, *The Nature of Fascism* (London, 1993); Philip Coupland, 'The Blackshirted Utopians', *Journal of Contemporary History*, Vol.33, No.2 (April 1998), pp.255–72.
5. Hölscher, op.cit., pp.5, 18–20, 27–30; *The Oxford English Dictionary*, Vol.XI, Oxford, 1933, p.486; *The Oxford English Dictionary* (second edition), Vol.XIX, Oxford, 1989, pp.370–1; Harold J. Laski, *A Grammar of Politics* (London, 1967; first published 1925) pp.212–16.
6. *Northampton Mercury and Herald*, 13 January 1933, p.6; Harold Macmillan, *Reconstruction: A Plea for a National Policy* (London, 1933), p.125.
7. 'Dystopia' was used in English in the modern sense in 1782 and the first use recorded of the related term 'dystopians' is by J.S. Mill in 1868. However, 'Dystopia' was not included in the 1933 edition of the *OED* and first emerged in the *Supplement* of 1972 (Patricia Köster, 'Dystopia: An Eighteenth Century Appearance', *Notes and Queries*, Vol.30 (new series), No.1, February 1983, pp.65–6; *OED* (second edition), Vol.V (Oxford, 1989), p.13. 'Cacotopia'—used by Jeremy Bentham in 1818 to communicate the same meaning—also failed to catch on. *OED* (second edition), Vol.II (Oxford, 1989), p.756.
8. Aldous Huxley, *Brave New World: A Novel*, Harmondsworth, 1955 (first published 1932), p.5.
9. William Henry Chamberlin, *A False Utopia: Collectivism in Theory and Practice*, London, 1937; Eugene Lyons, *Assignment in Utopia*, London, 1938; F.A. Hayek, *The Road to Serfdom*, London, 1944. For a contemporary variation on this theme see Correlli Barnett, *The Audit of War: The Illusion and Reality of Britain as Great Nation* (London, 1986).

10. Stafford Cripps, *The Struggle for Peace* (London, 1936), p.78; R.W.G. Mackay, *Peace Aims and the New Order* (London, 1941), p.130.
11. 'What is Really Happening?' *New Statesman and Nation*, Vol.2, 3 Oct. 1931, p.396.
12. C.R. Attlee, *The Labour Party in Perspective* (London, 1937), pp.26–30; A Group of Economists, Scientists and Technicians, *Britain Without Capitalists: A Study of What Industry in a Soviet Britain Could Achieve* (London, 1936); *Daily Worker*, 25 September 1936; *Left Review*, Vol.2, No.12, September 1936.
13. G.D.H. Cole, *The Intelligent Man's Guide Through World Chaos* (London, 1933), p.608; Paul Bloomfield, *Imaginary Worlds or the Evolution of Utopia* (London, 1932); 'Nightmares and Utopias', *New Clarion* Vol.2, 18 March 1933, p.292; T.N. Shane, 'On the Road to Utopia', *The Labour Magazine*, Vol.12, No.1, May 1933, pp.31–4; Nancy Adam, 'Switch to Utopia: How Electricity Helps the Modern Housewife', *Labour*, Vol.2, No.4, December 1934, p.81; 'England of the Future', *Northampton Chronicle and Echo*, 29 March 1934, p.7.
14. Oscar Wilde, *Plays, Prose Writings and Poems* (London, 1930), p.270; Harold J. Laski, 'Choosing the Planners', in G.D.H. Cole, et al., *Plan for Britain: A Collection of Essays prepared for the Fabian Society* (London, 1943), p.125.
15. Hugh Dalton, *Practical Socialism For Britain* (London, 1935), p.27; E.F.M. Durbin, *The Politics of Democratic Socialism: An Essay on Social Policy* (London, 1940), p.295; John Strachey, *Why You Should Be A Socialist* (London, 1944), p.77.
16. Common Wealth, *Common Wealth and the New Year* (1944), pp.7–8; Richard Acland, *What It Will Be Like in the New Britain* (London, 1942); idem., *Questions and Answers from Common Wealth Meetings*, 1944, p.79.
17. Aneurin Bevan, 'Plan for Work', in G.D.H. Cole, et al., *Plan for Britain: A Collection of Essays prepared for the Fabian Society* (London, 1943), pp.46–7; Julian Huxley, *Democracy Marches* (London, 1941), p.125.
18. Barbara Wootton, 'A Plague on all your Isms', *The Political Quarterly*, Vol.13, 1942, pp.44–56; Leonard Woolf, 'Utopia and Reality', *The Political Quarterly*, Vol.11, 1940, pp.167–82.
19. I.O. Evans, *The World of To-morrow: A Junior Book of Forecasts* (London, 1933); idem., 'London—What Might Be', *The New Clarion*, Vol.4, 6 January 1934, p.74; *Tribune*, 12 March 1937, p.13.
20. G.R. Mitchison, *The First Worker's Government; or, New Times for Henry Dubb*, London, 1934, p.6, p.13; my emphases.
21. Ethel Mannin, *Bread and Roses: An Utopian Survey and Blue Print*, London, 1944, p.8.
22. Emmanuel Shinwell, *The Britain I Want*, London, 1943; George Lansbury, *My England*, London, 1934; James Maxton, *If I Were Dictator*, London, 1935.
23. Attlee, op.cit., p.137, pp.163–4; T.W. Mercer, *Towards the Co-operative Commonwealth*, Manchester, 1936, p.201, pp.206–7.
24. Labour Party, *The Colonial Empire*, London, 1933, p.5.
25. *Daily Herald*, 23 May 1945, p.3; Stafford Cripps, *Toward Christian Democracy*, London, 1945, p.18.
26. British Library of Political and Economic Science, Miscellaneous Collection

723, Labour candidates' electoral addresses.
27. *New Clarion*, Vol. 4, 3 April 1934, p.194; Leah L'Estrange Malone, 'Forward to a Brave New World', *Labour Woman*, Vol.31, No.1, January 1943, p.5.
28. Karl Mannheim, *Ideology and Utopia*, New York, no date; first published in English 1936, pp.192–263. For critical discussion of Ideology and Utopia see Levitas, op.cit., ch.3; Krishan Kumar, *Utopianism*, Milton Keynes, 1991, pp.91–3; Alexander von Schelting, 'Ideologie und Utopie', *American Sociological Review*, Vol.1, No.4, August 1936, pp.664–74; Charles H. Wilson 'Ideology and Utopia', *Sociological Review*, Vol.29, No.4, October 1937, pp.414–19.
29. Derek Kahn, 'The Social Roots of Thought', *Left Review*, Vol.3, No.1, February 1937, pp.55–7. A.L. Rowse, 'Ideology and Utopia' *Political Quarterly*, Vol.8, 1937, pp.611–13. Harold J. Laski, 'Origins of Utopia' *New Statesman and Nation*, Vol.12, 14 November 1936, pp.778–9; my emphasis.
30. E.H. Carr, *The Twenty Years' Crisis* (London, 1939). Charles Jones 'Carr, Mannheim, and a Post-positivist Science of International Relations', *Political Studies*, Vol. XLV, 1997, pp.232–46.
31. Beilharz, op cit., pp.51–8.
32. Fred Henderson, *The Socialist Goal* (London, 1932), pp.3, 7; The same material appeared very little changed as *Planning or Chaos?* (London, 1938).
33. *Challenge,* Vol.3, No.6, February 1937, p.6; R. Page Arnot, *William Morris: A Vindication* (London, 1934), 'Immediate Programme or Social-Democratic Utopia', *Labour Monthly*, Vol.22, No.6, June 1940, CPGB, *Draft Programme*, 1939, p.15.
34. R.N. Berki, *Insight and Vision: The Problems of Communism in Marx's Thought* (London, 1983), pp.16–22. On Marxism and utopianism see also Bertell Ollman, 'Marx's Vision of Communism: A Reconstruction', *Critique*, No.8, Summer 1977, pp.4–41; Hölscher, op.cit., pp.27–30; Steven Lukes, 'Marxism and Utopianism', pp.153–67 in Peter Alexander and Roger Gill (eds), *Utopias* (London, 1984); Vincent Geoghegan, *Utopianism and Marxism* (London, 1987); Levitas, op.cit., ch.2.
35. E.P. Thompson, *William Morris: Romantic to Revolutionary* (London, 1977), pp.787–8.
36. *Daily Worker*, 19 January 1935, p.5; on aspects of CPGB utopianism, see: Raphael Samuel, 'The Lost World of British Communism', *New Left Review*, No.154, November-December 1985, pp.3–53; idem., 'Staying Power: The Lost World of British Communism', *New Left Review*, No.156, March—April 1986, pp.63–113; idem., 'Class Politics: The Lost World of British Communism', *New Left Review*, No.165, October 1987, pp.12–91; Nina Fishman, *The British Communist Party and the Trade Unions 1933–45*, Aldershot, 1995.
37. John Langdon-Davies, *A Short History of the Future*, London, 1936; 'Things to Come', *Challenge*, Vol.3, No. 1, 2 January 1937, p.6 (my emphasis); *Left Review,* Vol.2, No.15, December 1936, p.840.
38. Alan Hutt, 'Science and Society', *Labour Monthly*, Vol.21, No.5, May 1939, pp.319–20; J.D. Bernal, *The Social Function of Science*, London, 1939, p.346;

Christopher Caudwell, 'H.G. Wells: A Study in Utopianism', in *Studies in a Dying Culture*, London, 1938; pp.72–3.
39. A.J. Williams, *Labour and Russia: The Attitude of the Labour Party to the USSR, 1924–1934*, Manchester, 1989.
40. John Strachey, *The Theory and Practice of Socialism*, London, 1936, pp.275–8, 370; see also Hymie Lee, 'Our Propaganda', Discussion Vol.2, No.7, December 1937, pp.5–6; Christopher Caudwell, *Illusion and Reality: A Study of the Sources of Poetry* (London, 1973, first published 1937), p.90.
41. *Daily Worker*, 22 October 1931.
42. *Our Country*, Moscow, 1937, p.7; Pat Sloan, *Soviet Democracy*, London, 1937, p.288; Sydney Webb and Beatrice Webb, *Soviet Communism: A New Civilisation?*, 1935; Hewlett Johnson, *The Socialist Sixth of the World* (London, 1941, first published 1939), p.384; *Challenge*, Vol.2, No.8, August 1936, p.8; CPGB, *For Soviet Britain: The Programme of the Communist Party adopted at the XIII Congress February 2nd 1935* (London, 1935); for a Marxist-Leninist commentary on the history of the utopian literary genre in England and the USSR as utopia see A.L. Morton, *The English Utopia* (London, 1952).
43. *Challenge*, Vol.4, No.43, 5 November 1938; Stites, op.cit.; Geoghegan, op.cit., ch.5; George Orwell, *The Road to Wigan Pier* (London, 1937), p.240.
44. J. Allen Skinner 'A Plea for Utopianism', *Left*, No.99, January 1945, pp.303–6. On the relationship of ends and means for a CPGB authority see K.S. Shelvankar's response to Aldous Huxley's thesis on the subject (*Ends and Means: An Enquiry into the Nature of Ideals and into the Methods employed for their Realization*, London, 1937): *Ends and Means: A Critique of Social Values*, London, 1938.
45. The 'end of history' thesis is probably most associated with Francis Fukuyama ('The End of History?', *The National Interest*, Summer 1989, p.18; idem., *The End of History and the Last Man* (London, 1992). For a discussion of Fukuyama and post-modern and other views of society as post-utopian see Krishan Kumar, 'The End of Socialism? The End of Utopia? The End of History?' in K. Kumar, and S. Bann, *Utopias and the Millennium*, 1993; idem., 'Apocalypse, Millennium and Utopia Today' in M. Bull (ed.), *Apocalypse Theory and the Ends of the World* (Oxford, 1995).
46. Skinner, op.cit., p.306.

The Way the Future Was
Maureen Speller

In a sharp satire on science fictional visions of the future, William Gibson concludes, rather sadly:

> The Thirties dreamed white marble and slipstream chrome, immortal crystal and burnished bronze, but the rockets on the covers of the Gemsback pulps had fallen on London in the dead of night, screaming. After the war, everyone had a car—no wings for it—and the promised superhighway to drive it down, so that the sky itself darkened, and the fumes ate the marble and pitted the miracle crystal...[1]

The future conceived in science fiction stories rarely stands the test of quotidian reality. But then, science fiction is not in the business of predicting the future, and never has been. J. G. Ballard once remarked that science fiction was the best way of writing about the present, and most of the futures of science fiction are indeed best seen as mirrors of the author's present.

This is clear in the origins of the genre. The earliest direct precursor of science fiction is almost certainly Thomas More's *Utopia* (1516), in which he proposes an ideal, supposedly perfect society as a parallel to England under its new king (the island of Utopia is an almost exact mirror-image of England). Far from extolling the perfection of Utopia, however, More's book is, in fact, an attack upon it, for this is a land without Christianity: 'That is why they encourage euthanasia, condone divorce and harbour a multiplicity of religious beliefs'—all of which actions were considered dreadful by More himself and by Catholic Europe.[2] There is an element of the book in which More is laying out good practices that his monarch might follow, but in the main this is not an idealised portrait of the future but a warning of how the present might be without the good offices of the Catholic Church.

Over the next three hundred years numerous authors wrote stories which featured devices later associated with science fiction. The wondrous lands across the sea—common while America was itself a new-found land, pregnant with all sorts of possibilities of perfection—turned into lands rather further afield as the new colonies were settled, and we get instead a succession of journeys to the moon and the sun. Examples are many, and include *Somnium* (1634) by Johannes Kepler, *Other Worlds: The Comical History of the States and Empires of the Moon and Sun* (1657–62) by Cyrano de Bergerac, and *The Consolidator or Memoirs of Sundry Transactions from the World of the Moon* (1705) by Daniel Defoe. What they have in common is that none is intended seriously as a portrait of the future, or even as a realistic expectation of travel to other worlds (in Francis Godwin's *The Man in the Moone, or A Discourse of a Voyage Thither* by Domingo Gonsales, the *Speedy Messenger* (1638) the journey is accomplished in a vehicle drawn by wild geese). Rather, they are political satires suggesting better forms of governance (or, more typically, discreetly criticising existing modes of government) arising from the uncertainties of the wars, civil strife, religious persecution and idealistic communities of the age.

During the eighteenth century this political and religious turmoil was replaced by the Industrial Revolution: the drift of workers to the cities, the development of new modes of transport (first the canals, then the railways), the invention of new machines with the consequent threat to livelihoods, and the rise of a new monied class with increased leisure. It was in this atmosphere, and particularly under the patronage of this new aristocracy, that a new way of looking at the world developed in the form of Romanticism. The Romantic imagination found the sublime in wild places, in storms, in ancient ruins, and it was out of this morbid aspect of Romanticism that the Gothic emerged, in novels such as *The Castle of Otranto* (1765) by Horace Walpole, *Vathek* (1786) by William Beckford, *The Mysteries of Udolpho* (1794) by Ann Radcliffe and *The Monk* (1796) by Matthew Lewis. Here, the dark stuff of dreams, the shadow of the sublime, was discovered amid crumbling castles, rocky promontories, ghost-ridden abbeys. The Romantic in general and the Gothic in particular stood in direct contrast to the experience of a population now crowding into insanitary cities, who saw in desolate countryside a setting for hard labour rather than transcendent experience. There was, particularly in the love of ruins, a sense that the Gothic was backward-looking, but in one novel the moods and manners of the Gothic were harnessed not to shadows from the past but to fears for the future.

Frankenstein, or The Modern Prometheus (1818) by Mary Shelley clearly shares many of the tropes of the Gothic, from its wild settings (high in the Alps or deep in the Arctic wastes) to its evocation of emotions of pity and terror to its very prose style. Nevertheless, the novel grows out of the scientific experiments of the age, particularly the discovery of galvanism. Victor Frankenstein proceeds not by dark, mysterious means but by cold, scientific logic. It is this that has caused Frankenstein to be acclaimed the first science fiction novel.[3] Again, however, although it is a novel filled with warnings about what science may bring about (warnings so potent that Frankenstein continues to be a convenient shorthand for all our fears about scientific advance) it is not a novel about the future but about the present. Mary Shelley's later novel, *The Last Man* (1826), is specifically set in the future—it tells of humankind wiped out by plague at the end of the twenty-first century, setting the tone for a strand of catastrophe novels that includes *After London* (1885) by Richard Jefferies, *Earth Abides* (1949) by George R. Stewart, *The Day of the Triffids* (1951) by John Wyndham, and that continues to the present day in such novels as *A Scientific Romance* (1997) by Ronald Wright. Although this form of science fiction would come to be used to express a genuine post-war fear of the atomic threat—notably in novels such as *On the Beach* (1957) by Nevil Shute and *Golden Days* (1987) by Carolyn See, or television films such as *The Day After* (1983) and *Threads* (1985)—it rarely presented a clear or intentional vision of the future. Rather, the isolation of a few characters, just as they might be isolated on a desert island in Daniel Defoe's *Robinson Crusoe* (1719) or William Golding's *Lord of the Flies* (1954), allowed a similar isolation of moral intent. All too often, in Mary Shelley as in most of her successors, wiping out the entire human race did not entail a horrifying glimpse of our future but was a convenient way of having just a few characters who might express her moral point that much more clearly.

In so far as any science fiction during the nineteenth century provided a glimpse of the future, it was done with satirical intent that was inextricably tied to the present. Perhaps the most blatant example of this is to be found in the welter of stories prophesying war that began to appear in the 1870s and continued right up to the First World War. These (the finest example is *The Battle of Dorking* (1871) by George T. Chesney) had no purpose other than to proclaim England's lack of military preparedness in the face of Germany's unification, and its unexpectedly quick defeat of France in the Franco-Prussian War of 1870–71, though it is interesting to note that very similar stories with very similar intent were appearing in France, Germany and the USA at around the same time. Others viewed the future in a more benign light. In *News from Nowhere* (1890), for instance, William Morris probably did imagine he was giving us a genuine glimpse of the future in his rather anodyne vision of peace and plenty once the socialist ideal has been established across the world, yet his was a vision as closely tied to the concerns and interests and hopes of its moment as Chesney's.

Into this milieu emerged perhaps the most inventive writer that science fiction has yet produced, H.G. Wells. In a series of novels, beginning most dramatically with his very first, *The Time Machine* (1895), Wells established the themes and many of the devices that science fiction continues to explore to this day. As with so much science fiction, both before and since, Wells's work was rarely set in the future, but when he did so he looked ahead with a boldness that had not previously been seen. *The Time Machine*, for instance, takes us to the very moment when, in an entropic universe, all life on Earth comes to its natural end. But his most lasting vision of the future comes in a different part of that same short novel when we see the beautiful but ineffectual Eloi and the brutish Morlocks and discover, with a shock, that these are both descendants of modern humanity. How they are descended—and how the Eloi and the Morlocks reflect Wells's socialism more than any genuine attempt to portray the future—is best described with reference to one of his lesser-known stories, 'A Story of the Days to Come' (1897), which was clearly intended as a stepping stone between his late-Victorian world and the far future of the Eloi and the Morlocks. In this story, written curiously in a future tense by a writer specifically looking forward from Victorian England, we see a time, some centuries hence, in which the rich lead an effortless life surrounded by astonishing conveniences in beautiful domed cities. But their luxury and indolence is gained at the expense of those without wealth, who are confined literally under the cities where their labour is dark and brutal. Though it is never stated, we are surely meant to see in this division of mankind, the evolution of the Eloi and the Morlocks, so that this story and *The Time Machine* both become tracts urging support for equality, the nobility of labour and the like.

Wells's other great contribution to our vision of the future came at the end of his career in his sprawling late novel, *The Shape of Things to Come* (1933), and more particularly in the film version, *Things to Come* (1936). Most of the novel, which starts with the First World War and extends over several centuries, traces the birth of a benign world state through the traumas of war and destruction, but in its final passages, particularly in the film, it presents an idyllic, romantic image of an aseptic world of graceful spires and domes occupied by peaceful, high-minded people in togas and sandals. The portrait of the near-future which occupies the bulk of the novel comes as close to genuine prediction as anything Wells wrote and provides a chilling view of the onset and course of the Second World War which, though it varies in detail from what happened gets the broad sweep of history roughly right.

Like the work of Chesney before him, but with a far more careful and accurate working out of consequences from trends already visible, this part of the book is a political warning but as it develops into an idealised picture of a world state so it turns, like *News from Nowhere* before it, into an anodyne expression of current hopes and dreams more than a serious portrayal of any possible future.

American dream

The glittering spires and startling glass and chrome interiors that are the most powerful images of the future to emerge from the film of *Things to Come* are not an isolated vision. Clearly intended to provide a dramatic and hope-inspiring contrast to the narrow terraces and dark rooms that were familiar to most people at that time, particularly as the Depression was biting, these images fit neatly with other views of the future that were common at the time, the views displayed by American artist Frank R. Paul on the covers of American pulp magazines or in films like *Metropolis* (1926), the views satirised by William Gibson in *The Gemsback Continuum*. This is a vision of the future that is typical of science fiction, particularly American science fiction, from the days of the Gemsback pulps into the 1950s. The bulk of the science fiction written at this time was deeply conservative in character and tone. Although it offered a dramatic view of the future, from an America only a few years hence to a humanity that is spread across the cosmos, the prevailing impetus is the fulfilment of the American dream. Heroes are, almost invariably, white, male and American (if they differ from this pattern in any way—as, for example, when we discover midway through Robert A. Heinlein's gung-ho espousal of American military might in *Starship Troopers* (1959) that the protagonist is black—they inevitably support and represent white, male, American behaviour patterns, beliefs and ideals). The most common figure in American science fiction of this period is the competent hero, the lone man who, through superior strength, firepower or knowledge defeats the enemy and restores the old order. This figure has his analogue in American crime fiction of the period (the private eye in a seedy world who alone represents honour and goodness) In cowboy books and films such as Owen Wister's *The Virginian* (1902), the lone silent hero who becomes involved in the range wars of the 1880s on the side of vested interest, the cattle barons, is the ancestor of Clint Eastwood's icy killer in *A Fistful of Dollars* (1964). The scope of science fiction, however, allowed the writers of this period, popularly known as the 'Golden Age', to take on a broader canvas: Isaac Asimov's *Foundation Trilogy* (*Foundation* [1951], *Foundation and*

Empire [1952] and *Second Foundation* [1953]) uses *The Decline and Fall of the Roman Empire* as the model for a story sequence that covers thousands of years as a galactic society falls to outside forces but is restored thanks to a secret foundation that is the creation of one man. Thus the competent man can be the hero of stories on a scale impossible in any other genre.

Though most of the American science fiction of this period between the First World War and the 1950s is set hundreds if not thousands of years in the future, and often on worlds far from our own, the future is still clearly American. This was a period in which America was at the peak of its power and its confidence—victorious in two world wars, the greatest economic power in the world, the leading atomic power—and it saw no reason why that state of affairs should change. If world Governments were envisaged, they were centred on Washington. If a hero of the future was to arise he had to bear a good old American name (conversely, villains and mad dictators tended to have foreign-sounding names). The architecture among which this hero moved was clearly built on the American model, with soaring skyscrapers the norm. Between these towers would flit not cars but personal aircars, everyone enjoying unlimited power with no pedestrians to be seen, no downtrodden masses. The paraphernalia of this strangely uniform future was little more than a slight glamorising of the labour-saving devices that were even then pouring out of American factories. By the 1950s, American advertising was presenting a promise of a future that was kitted out almost exactly the way that science fiction stories of the day were kitted out. This was a vibrant, optimistic time where the future held nothing but glorious promise in which we would have all the goodies that are coming on line now, only more so. The future, as it was seen not just by American science fiction writers but by most Americans of the period, was very definitely American.

British writers

Only in Britain did the future look a little less rosy. British scientific romances of the 1930s tended to pessimism. At a time when war clouds were gathering in the Far East, Spain and over Nazi Germany, when the devastation of the First World War was still fresh in people's minds, and when the Jarrow March was highlighting the appalling suffering brought on by the Depression, it would have been hard to imagine that the future held any great promise. Neil Bell's *The Seventh Bowl* (1930) predicted the Gas War of 1940, John Gloag's *Tomorrow's Yesterday* (1932) compared the destructiveness of human civilisation unfavourably to a new race evolved from cats, and

Katharine Burdekin's *Swastika Night* (1937) looked forward to a Nazi dominated future in which women would be used as breeding animals. Perhaps the most pessimistic vision of all, however, was provided by Olaf Stapledon, the most influential figure in the history of British science fiction, after Wells. In *Last and First Men* (1930) he showed that humanity was no more than an insignificant speck in the vastness of space and time by constructing a devastating history of the future which begins with the destruction of our own civilisation, then follows the rise and inevitable fall of future races of men across two billion years. At the heart of the book is a spiritual quest that remains unfulfilled, even when we rise to the wisdom of the *Eighteenth Men*, and the result is an awesome but pitiless work.

Nothing of such a scale has ever been attempted again in science fiction, but the pessimism for the future remained as a characteristic of British science fiction after the Second World War. Though Britain emerged victorious from the war, it was at a cost. The economy was devastated and rationing and strict government controls that lasted into the 1950s meant that the country saw few fruits of victory. The empire, which had provided a cheap source of imports, a ready market for exports and convenient jobs for a significant portion of our population, was breaking up, starting with the most costly loss of all, the independence of India. British fiction of the period was suffused with the moods generated by these circumstances, and science fiction was no exception. The dominant mode of British science fiction throughout the 1950s and into the 1960s was what Brian Aldiss has termed the 'cosy catastrophe',[4] in which a force from outside tears apart some corner of rural England (usually physically as well as socially) and a handful of characters must then struggle to survive and to reestablish their traditional values.

The most significant British science fiction writer to emerge at this time, however, had a very different perspective on the future. Arthur C. Clarke derived his vision from Olaf Stapledon and his tone of voice from his American contemporaries, but in one respect he harked back directly to science fiction's Romantic, Gothic origins. He saw the future as a way to the sublime: what we achieve by going out into space is transcendence. This is prefigured in a number of early works, notably *Childhood's End* (1953) and *The City and the Stars* (1956), but it is most clearly shown in his most famous work, *2001, A Space Odyssey* (1968), in which the astronaut seeking alien contact is transformed into the Star Child, signalling the birth of a new, transcendent form of humanity. Clarke may not have been the first science fiction writer to use such an idea, but he followed it through more consistently in all his work than anyone else, and by so doing set the tone for much of the far future science fiction that has followed. Nowadays, transcendence has become a popular underlying current in views of mankind's eventual future among the stars in works as varied as *Eternal Light* (1991) by Paul J. McAuley and *A Fire Upon the Deep* (1992) by Vernor Vinge.

New Wave

The 1960s brought a radical change in science fiction on both sides of the Atlantic, though the continuing differences between British and American science fiction are disguised by the fact that the new movement was called the 'New Wave' in both places. In Britain, post-war austerity had turned into affluence, and science fiction was becoming associated with both the literary avant-garde and the youth culture of the day. The catastrophe story still remained the dominant mode in British science fiction, but now it was transformed by drug references, the quest for inner space, and dynamic leftwing questioning of the political status quo that had been virtually unknown in science fiction for decades. Led by the magazine *New Worlds* under the editorship of Michael Moorcock, the science fiction of writers such as Brian Aldiss, L.G. Ballard, John Brunner, Christopher Priest and M. John Harrison became experimental and challenging studies of the nature of identity and the place of the individual in society. Almost without exception these stories took place in a radically transformed here and now. For a while, at least, the future and outer space ceased to be of interest to science fiction writers.

While the New Wave in Britain was typified by literary experimentalism, in America it was marked by a dramatic iconoclasm. Although here, too, science fiction was associated with the youth culture, its new young writers were spurred by the Vietnam War which led to a radical questioning of the conservative values that had until then been an accepted part of American science fiction. Typified by the anthology *Dangerous Visions* (1967) edited by Harlan Ellison, in which the contributors were deliberately challenged to overturn taboos, the new generation of science fiction writers such as Robert Silverberg, Samuel R. Delany, Roger Zelazny and Ursula K. Le Guin wrote about drugs, sex and politics in a way that was designed to outrage their forebears. This was a time of immense controversy in American science fiction, in which attitudes towards the Vietnam War were routinely split along generational lines, and in which the great names in science fiction from the 1940s and 1950s regularly denounced the work of their younger followers (although some of the older generation of writers—notably Theodore Sturgeon and Philip K. Dick—were more than happy to embrace the work and the attitudes of the new generation). American New Wave writers wrote about the future far more than their British contemporaries, but it was a very different future from what had gone before. The chrome was now tarnished, the graceful towers were toppling and there were fewer aircars and more pedestrians. If not exactly pessimistic, American science fiction was certainly less optimistic than it had been. In *The World Inside* (1971) Robert Silverberg sees the high-rise towers of the future not as a glamorous vision but as a setting for social decay, while in *Aye and Gomorrah* (1967) Samuel R. Delany uses his astronauts of the future to question sexual identity and values.

As ever, these visions of the future are really reflections of the present, or sometimes even the past. Philip K. Dick is one of the finest and most important science fiction writers of the last half century, but in novels of the future, such as *Our Friends from Frolix 8* (1970), behind the futuristic hardware, he paints a picture of a society that is identical in almost every respect to the society of California in the 1950s which he portrayed in his mainstream novels such as *Mary and the Giant* (written 1953–5, not published until 1987) or *The Broken Bubble* (written 1956, published 1988).

Feminist writers

Perhaps the most radical change to science fiction in the 1960s, however, was the emergence of a new generation of women writers, who began to use science fiction to express feminist ideals. There had always been women writing science fiction: Mary Shelley, Katharine Burdekin, C. L. Moore, Margaret St Clair among others, though the genre had always been heavily dominated by male writers (to the extent that Burdekin and St Clair used male pseudonyms for at least some of their work, Murray Constantine and Idris Seabright respectively, and Moore, as well as signing her work with just her initials, also used the pseudonym Lewis Padgett, which she shared with her husband Henry Kuttner). Such was the situation that in 1960 Kingsley Amis could write: 'Though it may go against the grain to admit it, science-fiction writers are evidently satisfied with the sexual status quo.'[5] There were, however, male writers sympathetic to a feminist perspective, particularly Theodore Sturgeon author of *Venus Plus X* (1960) and *If All Men Were Brothers Would You Let One Marry Your Daughter?* (1967) and John Wyndham who, in *Consider Her Ways* (1956) had presented a world without men which did not automatically assume that in such a situation things would fall apart. Now, however, more and more women writers were finding that science fiction allowed them to express feminist ideas more easily than other forms of literature. Prominent among these were Ursula K. Le Guin, whose *The Left*

Hand of Darkness (1969) introduced a world whose androgynous inhabitants are able to take on either male or female sexual characteristics, and Alice Sheldon, writing as James Tiptree Jr., whose *The Women Men Don't See* (1973) gently suggested that males and females are in fact alien to each other.

Inevitably, feminist writers using the conventions of science fiction produced very different visions of the future. Most were forms of utopia, but they tended to be ambiguous at best. Both Marge Piercy, in *Woman on the Edge of Time* (1976), and Josephine Saxton, in *Queen of the States* (1986), have their female protagonists imprisoned in a mental institution, as if being a woman in contemporary society is a form of madness. From this madness emerge visions of a feminist future that is automatically seen as a more rational way of life, though there is also the ambiguous possibility that the vision is itself a part of the madness. The ambiguity of such utopias is exemplified by Ursula K. Le Guin's fable, *The Ones Who Walk Away From Omelas* (1973), in which a seemingly perfect society is examined in detail until we discover the dark secrets that allows the society to operate, and then meet those who walk away from Omelas, unable to bear the cost of perfection.

As with most visions of the future, feminist science fiction was a reflection of the hopes and aspirations of the present. Feminist utopias, therefore, tended to be fiercest when arguments for female equality were at their most impassioned. For a time, between the mid-1970s and the late 1980s, feminist science fiction almost constituted a separate sub-genre and a number of feminist and lesbian presses created their own science fiction imprints. During the 1990s most of these have fallen silent. That does not mean that feminists have stopped writing science fiction, Sheri Tepper in particular continues to express sometimes strident feminist views in her science fiction, such as Gibbon's *Decline and Fall* (1996), sometimes at the risk of seriously unbalancing her fiction. But the visions of the future expressed by feminist writers have changed, so that the British writer, Gwyneth Jones, for instance, can subsume the feminist experience in a powerful and moving vision of the colonial experience from the standpoint of the colonised rather than the colonisers. In her trilogy, *White Queen* (1991), *North Wind* (1994) and *Phoenix Café* (1997), she tells of an Earth colonised by aliens whose gender is ambiguous; the experiences of the oppressed and of women become identified, and then confused with searching questions about social, political and sexual identity. Such a perception of the future suggests that in the present issues of sexuality have become part of wider political concerns.

Cyberpunk

At the same time that feminist science fiction was developing its own distinctive voice, another vision of the future was emerging from the so-called 'cyberpunk' writers. Led by William Gibson, Bruce Sterling and Pat Cadigan this was a new generation of primarily American writers who embraced many of the science fiction traditions that dated back to the 'Golden Age' of the 1940s and 1950s, but who gave them a radical, streetwise gloss that incorporated an enthusiasm for the possibilities offered by computer-based technology. Politically, their vision of the future was radical in that they no longer perceived America as central in the global power networks of the future. In fact, this is a science fiction that is built upon the tiger economies of Asia, and in novels from William Gibson's *Neuromancer* (1984) to Pat Cadigan's *Tea From an Empty Cup* (1998) Japan is central to their notion of the future. Technologically, they anticipate an ever greater reliance on computers in all their forms, to the extent that distinctions between machine and man become blurred and disturbing.

Cyberpunk, as a distinct form of science fiction, did not really last into the 1990s, but the visions of the future it engendered still underlie most of the science fiction being written today. Technological science fiction is as optimistic about the future as at any time since the 1950s. Although the fiction contains as many warnings as celebrations, it still tends to be excited by the possibilities of computer technology, of nanotechnology (for instance in Greg Bear's *Queen of Angels* (1990), of exploring and developing other worlds as in Kim Stanley Robinson's trilogy *Red Mars* (1992), *Green Mars* (1993) and *Blue Mars* (1996), and of genetic engineering as in Paul J. McAuley's *Fairyland* (1996). At the same time the social concerns generated particularly by feminist science fiction have had their own distinct effect, so that visions of the future today tend to far greater equality in social, sexual and racial terms. Yet these positive attitudes towards the future don't necessarily make for an optimistic literature. British science fiction continues to view the future with as much doubt as it has ever done. The biological wonders displayed in McAuley's *Fairyland* are also equated with political and social disintegration; virtual reality, in Christopher Priest's *The Extremes* (1998) can lead us to question our own reality; and even that most positive of science fictional adventures, space exploration, is conjoined with the extinction of humanity in Stephen Baxter's *Titan* (1997). What is perhaps new is that this lack of optimism is starting to be felt in American science fiction also, so that Sheri Tepper's *The Family Tree* envisages a far future in which humanity has been reduced to beasts of burden, while Bruce Sterling's *Distraction*

(1999) portrays a near-future America that has already undergone political and economic disintegration and now appears to be on the point of breaking up as a country; it is as close to a British catastrophe novel as American science fiction has ever produced.

Notes

1. William Gibson, 'The Gemsback Continuum' (1981), collected in *Burning Chrome* (Gollancz, 1986), p.32. The Gemsback of the title is Hugo Gemsback (1884–1967), who introduced what he called 'scientifiction' stories into the magazines of popular mechanics he edited in the early years of the century, as a way of proselytising the wonderful future he believed technology would bring.
2. Peter Ackroyd, *The Life of Thomas More* (Chatto & Windus, 1998), pp.168–9. Ackroyd's reading of *Utopia* is not necessarily the most common one, but it is convincing. As he goes on to say: 'Utopia is an ambivalent and ambiguous work in which various absurdities, for example, are paraded in the most apparently innocent and unsatirical manner. But it also harbours various contradictions which render the account of Hythlodaeus very suspect indeed. The counter-argument, the case against *Utopia* in effect, is internalised within the narrative itself' (p.170).
3. This view first gained wide currency in *Billion Year Spree* by Brian Aldiss (Weidenfeld & Nicolson, 1973), later expanded as *Trillion Year Spree* by Brian Aldiss with David Wingrove (Gollancz, 1986) and is now generally accepted. However, identification of the first science fiction novel or the first science fiction writer depends largely on how science fiction is defined, so convincing arguments can be made for a wide range of other founding fathers, from More's *Utopia* to H.G. Wells and Hugo Gemsback.
4. Aldiss coined this term in *Billion Year Spree* specifically as a description of the work of John Wyndham. More recent commentators have suggested that this is a misnomer, and that Wyndham's work was more radical than the safe, middle-class values that Aldiss ascribes to them.
5. Kingsley Amis, *New Maps of Hell* (Gollancz, 1961). Originally delivered as a series of lectures at Princeton, this was the first book-length critical study of science fiction to be published.
6. This essay would have been impossible without the use of a number of invaluable reference sources, in particular *The Science Fiction Encyclopedia* (Orbit, 1993), edited by John Clute and Peter Nicholls; *Science Fiction: The Illustrated Encyclopedia* by John Clute (Dorling Kindersley, 1995); and *A Very British Genre: A Short History of British Fantasy and Science Fiction* by Paul Kincaid, BSFA, 1995.

Theodore Rothstein and the Origins of the British Communist Party
David Burke and Fred Lindop

The Moscow connection

The relationship between the British left and Russia during the twentieth century has largely been seen as a one-way affair, where the domestic and foreign policy needs of Moscow came to determine the internal politics of the Communist Party of Great Britain (CPGB). At its most extreme is Henry Pelling's statement made in 1958 'that there can be few topics more worthy of exploration than the problem of how it came to pass, that a band of British citizens could sacrifice themselves so completely over a period of almost forty years to the service of a dictatorship in another country....'[1] Pelling's work betrays both a failure and a reluctance on his part to understand why it was that a political party advocating class unity and class struggle could appeal to a section of the British working-class in the first half of the twentieth century. Pelling, writing five years after the death of Stalin and two years after Khrushchev's speech to the 20th Congress of the Communist Party of the Soviet Union, portrayed British communists as lacking in independent thought and acting just like CPSU functionaries.

In 1969, in response to a growing academic and popular interest in marxism, a more sophisticated attempt was made to explain the apparent failure of British marxism. Walter Kendall's *The Revolutionary Movement in Britain 1900–1921* argued that the Communist Party of Great Britain (CPGB) was wholly an 'artificial creation'—the direct result of Moscow's intervention in British left-wing politics.[2] Essentially, Kendall argues that Lenin, by utilising leading figures in the Russian émigré community in Britain, manipulated individuals and groups by funding their organisations—the much-maligned 'Moscow Gold'. In this way, he was able to arrest the native development of British Marxism and set it off on a different course altogether. Crucial to Kendall's argument is the prominent role played by a Russian political émigré, Fyodor Aronovich Rotshstein (Theodore Rothstein) who had known

Lenin during his Iskra period in London (1902–03), and who in 1920 attached himself to the Russian Trading Delegation in London, from where he orchestrated the formation of a Communist Party sympathetic to Lenin's immediate foreign policy needs.[3] No doubt the subsequent political career of Theodore Rothstein in Moscow (not to mention the role played by his son Andrew in the CPGB) helped establish and maintain links between the British left and the CPSU, thereby influencing communist activity in Britain. But was Rothstein, who had been included in the British socialist movement since 1895, acting as the mouthpiece of Lenin in 1919–20 rather than the British revolutionary movement?

More recently, Martin Crick in his *The History of the Social-Democratic Federation* (1994), has also commented upon the historical roots of this relationship between Moscow and the British left, and questions the extent to which a native British Marxist tradition was challenged by the Bolshevik Revolution. However, while remaining unconvinced by Kendall's Machiavellian treatment of Rothstein, Crick nevertheless relies upon Kendall for his portrayal of Rothstein and the development of his politics. He thereby creates confusion when he comes to assess the legacy of the Social-Democratic Federation (SDF) for both British communism and other twentieth-century left-wing organisations. In essence in order to take issue with Kendall's assertion that a native British Marxist movement had developed around the legendary Clydeside figure John Maclean, Crick discards too readily the notion that revolutionary politics were a threat to the British State in the period 1915–19. Here Crick utilises Kendall's political portrait of Rothstein in order to demonstrate the looseness of Rothstein's political understanding of the revolutionary forces in both Russia and Britain.[4] Yet Bolshevism should not be seen as a monolithic organisation with a clear knowledge of what it intended to do, particularly in 1917:

> Rothstein was certainly a late convert to Bolshevism; for much of the period he supported the Menshevik position which opposed the war but doubted Russia's readiness for Socialism. His *Essays on War and Peace*, published by the BSP in 1917, called for a negotiated peace rather than an end to the war through Socialist revolution. He backed the entry of the Mensheviks into the Provisional Government and criticised the Leninite opposition to that. Rothstein was certainly to the right of Maclean prior to the Bolshevik Revolution, but Maclean was almost unique amongst British Socialists in his advocacy of 'revolutionary defeatism'. There was no clear picture of events in Russia and most British Socialists were reactive rather than creative in their policies.[5]

It is unquestionable that Rothstein played a crucial role in the negotiations leading up to the formation of the CPGB. He undoubtedly influenced the politics adopted by the party. But historians have hitherto been content to approach Rothstein as a post-1917 activist, and have ignored his earlier career. Both Crick and Kendall do make reference to his role in the SDF during the Boer War particularly in leading the SDF away from sectarianism, and into engagement with practical politics. But, by and large, his career as an active socialist in Britain between 1895 and 1917 has been largely ignored. In addition, while his subsequent career in Britain 1917–20 has been discussed, his career in the Soviet Union 1920–53 has also been neglected. In 1983 Lawrence & Wishart republished his *From Chartism to Labourism* first published in 1929 with an introduction by John Saville which outlined the main features of his career as a left-wing activist in Britain. The following year the *Dictionary of Labour Biography* published a short biography by Keith Nield; and in the same year Frank Cass published a book edited by John Slatter, entitled *From The Other Shore: Russian Political Emigrants in Britain, 1880–1917*; which among other chapters on Russian political émigrés active in the British radical and labour movements contained an article on Theodore Rothstein's career in the British labour movement.[6] A further work, Sharman Kadish's *Bolsheviks and British Jews: The Anglo-Jewish Community, Britain and the Russian Revolution* (1992) looked, as its title suggests, at the general impact of the Russian Revolution on Britain's Jewish community, but while looking at Rothstein and other Jewish left-wing activists from the standpoint of émigré politics amongst an immigrant group, Kadish did not emphasise Rothstein's position as a *British* socialist (our emphasis). This article, on the other hand, looks at the political career of Theodore Rothstein both as a Russian political émigré and as a British socialist whose influence on British Marxism was considerable.

Theodore Rothstein

Theodore Rothstein was born in Kovno, now Kaunas in Lithuania, on 26 February 1871. His father, an apothecary, had nurtured ambitions for his son as a medical doctor, and moved his family to Poltava in the Ukraine where Theodore attended the Gymnasium. His main interest, however, lay in applying Marxism to a study of classical literature. As a medical student he joined an illegal study group run by an exiled member of the Narodnaya Volya ('People's Will') terrorist organisation. The study circle read and discussed the works of Chernishevskii and Dobroliubov, and later the few Marxist texts that were beginning to circulate illegally: *Kommunisticheskii manifest* (*Communist Manifesto*), Engels's *Razvitie sotsializma ot utopii k nauke* (*Development of Socialism from Utopia to Science*), and parts of the first volume of *Kapital* (*Capital*). His political activities were brought to the attention of the local authorities and to avoid possible arrest Rothstein went into voluntary exile along with his family in 1891, following an anonymous tipoff 'that "TR had better get out."' The family moved first to Germany where an older brother Phoebus lived in Danzig. From there, in the same year, the family moved to Leeds, where Rothstein's father and Theodore's younger brother Albert ran a chemist's shop. Theodore was the only member of his family to become involved in politics and while in Leeds he acted as honorary secretary of the local branch of the Society of Friends of Russian Freedom (SFRF), and worked for the Russian Free Press Fund (RFPF) as a translator.[7] In 1893 he moved to London and began working on what was to be a Marxist history of Rome. He worked on this project for two years, studying in the British Museum; while doing so he was supported by his family. Although this work was never finished he published articles on Plato, Socrates, Alexander the Great, Julius Caesar, Demosthenes and Cicero in the Russian journal *Zhizn zamechatel'nikh lyudei* (*The Lives of Famous People*), and he also published an article on Roman poetry under the nom de plume E. Orlov in the journal *Zhizn'* (*Life*).[8]

Theodore Rothstein married in 1895; his wife Anna Kahan belonged to another politically active Jewish immigrant family. Her brother Boris and sister Zelda all became members of the SDF, Theodore, Anna and Boris joining the Whitechapel branch in 1895. In 1896 he resumed work as a translator and as a sub-editor for the journal of the SFRF *Free Russia*. This led to employment on Campbell-Bannerman's shortlived radical newspaper *The Tribune* as a 'sub', and then on the *Daily News* from 1907; an income supplemented by occasional articles for the *Manchester Guardian* on international affairs from 1911 onwards.[9]

His first article for the SDF paper *Justice* in 1896 engaged with the current debates in the socialist movement and attempted to offer a synthesis of the revolutionary and evolutionary methods of social progress. Rothstein argued that the two doctrines were not necessarily opposed to each other but were two sides of the same reality:

> we, at least the Social-Democrats, have outgrown to a very great extent this crude conception of revolution being a negation of evolution ... To our mind a revolution is as much a legitimate movement in the evolutionary process of development of an organism as that piecemeal slow, and often imperceptible change with which the idea of evolution is generally associated.[10]

Rothstein had, from the outset, taken up a position on revolutionary theory closely aligned with that of the Second International and SDF.

However, in May 1897, he published a critical history of the British labour movement in the *Social-Democrat* (discussion journal of the SDF) which clearly reflected the influence of his Russian experience. This led him to exaggerate the ease with which British socialists could assume the leadership of the working class, which he saw as being mainly a political struggle against a government and a Liberal Party divorced from the mainstream of British society, in much the same way as Tsarism controlled political life in Russia.[11]

Yet if Rothstein initially approached British working-class history with what many of his British contemporaries regarded as the arrogance of continental socialism, it was soon tempered by British conditions. During the engineers lock-out (July 1897–January 1898), Rothstein was made aware of the strong political ties existing between liberal-radicalism and the trade-union movement. In his first article on contemporary British issues, he pointed out that throughout the strike the liberal-radical bourgeoisie had offered a defence of the engineers while the social-democrats had failed to do so. This could only strengthen the hold of the Liberal Party on the political loyalties of the leading sections of the working class. Rothstein argued that socialists within the trade unions had to raise the dispute's political aspects:

> At the coming National Conference of the trade unions many Socialists of the SDF and the ILP will undoubtedly be present, and on them devolves the duty to present our case. Let them spare no efforts to put the present fight and the attitude assumed towards it by the middle class, in their proper light. Otherwise we in England shall have to do our work over again.[12]

However, although Rothstein was suggesting a change in attitude towards trade unionism, it still put the primacy of politics and political theory above the economic attachment of certain sections of the working class to sympathetic elements within the bourgeoisie. It was a simplistic view which led Rothstein to conclude that the working class in order to develop a sense of its own independent political identity, had merely to shrug off middle-class patronage and tutelage.

Against the Boer War

The outbreak of the Boer War in October 1899 confirmed Rothstein in this view. Rothstein's influence within the SDF, as both Crick and Kendall have pointed out, was greatly strengthened by his leading role in the agitation against the Boer War. His opposition, along with that of Belfort Bax, to the anti-semitism and pro-imperialist line of Hyndman and much of the SDF's old leadership rallied the majority of the party's rank and file. Bax and Rothstein began to develop a theoretical analysis of imperialism which the socialist movement then lacked. Rothstein argued that anti-war and anti-imperialist agitation provided an important opportunity to promote socialism to a wider audience among the still Liberal-oriented working class. He saw the failure by the liberal-radicals to develop an effective anti-war movement (because of their fear of splitting the Liberal Party) as a major opportunity for a real political advance by the SDF:

> Now is the psychological moment for which many of us have been on the look-out for the last ten or fifteen years; now is the time to get into line with the continental Socialists whose good fortune it is to have become the sole keepers and champions of Right a quarter of a century ago. The great obstacle in our way has been forcibly and in good time removed by the war; there is no one left to take the wind out of our sails any longer: Liberalism is dead and rotting in its grave.[13]

The following week, 14 April 1900, Rothstein was urging British social-democracy to cut all ties with liberal-radicalism. Two months later in the June 1900 edition of the *Social-Democrat* Rothstein repeated his argument, but in terms which chastised the SDF for what he saw as its sectarian laziness:

> ... we have been more of a sect than a party. We regarded the world with an eye, not so much of active participators, as of intelligent onlookers, and far from thinking to impress upon it our distinct personality, we contented ourselves with examining it from our particular standpoint. And that standpoint was especially adapted to estrange us from life.[14]

Rothstein's analysis of the anti-war agitation, therefore, was not simply concerned with achieving a more militant campaign; it also pointed to new opportunities for the socialist movement owing to a crisis in the Liberal Party. It also offered a criticism of SDF strategy that identified sectarianism as its major weakness. Rothstein's growing status in the SDF was reflected in his election to the Party's Executive in 1900; the following year he was re-elected with the highest vote.

Socialist disputes and socialist unity

Rothstein continued to play a leading role in the SDF (and the SDP as it became in 1907). In the Impossibilist controversy (1901–3), which saw a section of the Scottish membership condemn all contact with reformists or reformist bodies, Rothstein tried to bring the two strands of opinion together. The arguments between the two groups became particularly acute over Taff Vale. Rothstein's position was clear:

> In any country where Socialism is really synonymous with the working-class movement of the land, such a mean ... attack on trade unionism would have found the Socialists the first to take up the gauntlet and to initiate a campaign on behalf of the party attacked ... [15]

In a further article summarising the debate he took a middle course between what he described as 'the Scylla of boneless opportunism and the Charybdis of ossified impossibilism'.[16] Socialists, he argued, must support trade union candidatures on all labour matters; but on political questions they must reserve the right to act according to their own convictions. Rothstein was concerned not to alienate reformists with a policy that dismissed trade union candidatures out of hand; but he tried to win over the impossibilists by arguing that the external factors which had made possible the political and social alliance between the progressive bourgeoisie and trade unionists in the last century, no longer existed. His attempt to steer a middle course produced the basis of an SDF position on trade union candidatures, but it did not resolve the theoretical and practical impasse that was stifling the Party. Nor did it satisfy the impossibilists who were finally expelled in 1903.

During this time the SDF was again involved in unity proposals with the Independent Labour Party (ILP). Both the SDF and the ILP had suffered steep falls in membership in the years after 1897 and the right wing of the SDF saw socialist unity as a way of reversing the decline. Rothstein voted for unity at the 1902 SDF conference, without any great expectations; and when the ILP leadership contemptuously rejected the SDF approach, he sharply attacked the opportunism of Hardie and his associates. Accusing the ILP of 'rank opportunism—opportunism of principle as distinguished from that of tactics'—Rothstein saved his obloquy for the activities of Keir Hardie at a recent Newcastle meeting of the Labour Representation Committee

(LRC). At this meeting, Rothstein stated, Hardie had 'propounded the principle that the movement must be non-political'. He went on to censure Hardie for his activities at the February Guildhall meeting called to set up the National Unemployed Committee, where as chairman he had ignored SDF members wanting to speak. 'Mr. Keir Hardie,' Rothstein concluded, 'is fast becoming a "responsible statesman" who does not wish to give undue offence by obtruding everywhere his socialism.' That this was not a new development led Rothstein to ask why relations between the ILP leadership and its membership had not become strained. Many ILP members had always been attracted by the hope of socialist unity, at the heart of which lay the goal of some sort of link with the SDF. Earlier discussion on fusion in the 1890s had been undermined by the ILP's National Administrative Council (NAC). If, as some ILP members now claimed, they were in all essentials socialists, then it was their duty to resign from the ILP and join the SDF:

> The erratic ways of Mr. Keir Hardie and his satellites do not merely date from yesterday, and if the ILP is really a Socialist party, their ways should have proved by now a sufficiently strong strain upon the loyalty of the members to break it down. If it does not if these gentlemen are allowed to go on as before, then really I, for one, must assume that the party endorses their actions and that, consequently, as I said at the beginning, there are no two Socialist parties in England, which it is in the interests of the cause, desirable to see fused into one, but only one, the SDF, which must and shall remain alone.[17]

There was an ever-present emphasis in Rothstein's writings on the need for socialists to adopt a more openly Marxist standpoint on the question of socialist unity. Rothstein and the SDF executive insisted that socialism would not advance if they simply stole Liberal clothes; rather they had to stand on an independent understanding of class action.

1905 Revolution

What was to finally give a practical as opposed to an abstract quality to these developments was the outbreak of revolution in Russia in 1905. Rothstein's analysis of the Revolution owed much to his reading of British history, which had identified in the evolutionary tenets of British parliamentarism a potentially effective instrument for revolutionary change. A working-class political party could only succeed in parliament if it organised itself on a socialist basis, and opposed the liberal bourgeoisie. The dissolution of the Russian Duma in August 1906 confirmed Rothstein in this view, and encouraged him to see in any future Duma the development of a progressive, reforming body, capable of moving the Russian Revolution forward.[18]

Rothstein, along with Lenin, had remained throughout the revolutionary period unconvinced by Trotsky's arguments that Russia was on the brink of a proletarian, not a bourgeois, revolution, that would bring a workers' government to power. Like Lenin, Rothstein rejected Plekhanov's commitment to an alliance with the liberals in making the bourgeois revolution. He recognised the crucial revolutionary significance of the land question and peasant land hunger, but rejected Lenin's notion of an alliance between the proletariat and the peasantry which would carry through the bourgeois revolution. For Rothstein this problem was to be resolved by the proletariat extending the bourgeois revolution to the countryside and freeing the peasantry from the remnants of feudalism, thereby creating the conditions for capitalism in the countryside. With the subsequent spread of the class struggle to the peasantry Rothstein believed that the conditions would be created for a successful proletarian revolution in the future. For this reason Rothstein had begun to see the Duma as the legitimate expression of dissent in Russia. Its dissolution had coincided with the exhaustion of the revolution. What had been a year of continuous strikes and nervous tension ended in a state of physical collapse; henceforth, opposition in Russia would rely increasingly on constitutional forms of protest—seeking to influence and educate public opinion through a newly-promised State Duma to be convened in February 1907.[19]

Rothstein had earlier transferred his respect for the Duma in Russia to British parliamentary conditions, leading him to reassess the role of the British Labour Party as a potentially combative organisation in parliament. In an article entitled, 'Parliamentarianism and the Working Class', he commented upon the proposed resolution of the Labour Party for parliamentary representatives to become independent of conference decisions. His objection to this proposal was couched in language which drew its understanding from his analysis of the workings of the Russian Duma. The aforementioned resolution of the Parliamentary Labour Party, he argued, would be nothing less than the 'opportunist ... betrayal of the working class' brought forward 'under the pretext that a Member of Parliament is, in the first instance, responsible to his constituents.' This Rothstein argued, was a misguided notion: if a constituent returned a given candidate, then he had expressed his solidarity with that MP's programme and party, and not with an individual. If MPs were granted freedom for their actions and independence for their decisions, then political expediency would almost certainly encourage alliances with liberal-radical parties.[20]

While no doubt Rothstein had in mind Millerandism in France, he sought to challenge these tactics by applying what he saw as the role of the Russian Social-Democratic Labour Party (RSDLP) in the new Duma to British parliamentary conditions. Rothstein's starting point had been the irreconcilable antagonism between the proletariat and the bourgeoisie; this had to be built upon, both inside and outside of Parliament. Parliament on its own could neither revolutionise nor organise the forces of the proletariat, but it could serve as an instrument whereby the antagonism between the two groups could be fully exposed, enabling the proletariat to 'organise itself for the complete political and economic dispossession of the bourgeoisie.'[21] This, Rothstein felt, was the proper function of the Labour Party and parliamentarism for the British working class. On the other hand, to pursue the tactics advocated by its leaders would be merely to oversee the party's disintegration as a class organisation.

Militarism

From 1907 Rothstein was one of the leading figures in the labour movement defending the militarism and anti-militarism resolution adopted by the Stuttgart conference of the Second International. He found himself once again co-ordinating the opposition to Hyndman in the sphere of foreign policy. Hyndman, back again in the party leadership, was actively seeking to sabotage the Stuttgart resolution. His support for the Government's policy of isolating the Kaiser by constructing an alliance with France and the Tsar was particularly offensive to Rothstein who regarded any agreement with Tsarist Russia as an endorsement of reaction. Later Hyndman's support for the Triple Entente, with its anti-German bias, led him to speak out in favour of a bigger navy which the Tory Party and some of the press had forced the Government to accept. His articles in *Justice* and in the *Clarion* (whose editor Blatchford shared his hostility to German 'aggression') and later in the right wing *Morning Post*, continually threatened to undermine party unity and sour relations with the Second International. Hyndman had the support of most of the SDP's older leadership including the editor of *Justice*, Harry Quelch, and the general secretary of the party, H.W. Lee. The jingoistic nature of the 'big navy' campaign whipped up considerable anti-foreigner feeling and increased working-class support for the naval building programme. In an incisive article in *Justice*, Rothstein pointed out that the Tory slogan of 'We want eight and we won't wait' obscured the 'bourgeois party manoeuvres' behind the campaign. In order to contest the Liberal Party's policy of social reform and drive the Liberal free traders into financial bankruptcy, the Tory Party demanded an increase in armaments. 'It was very shrewdly calculated', Rothstein pointed out, that if most of the money available on the present system of taxation were spent on armaments, nothing would be left for the social reforms to which the Liberal Government stands pledged and the Tories would then come to power with a mandate to 'broaden the basis of taxation'. Naturally the cry was raised 'the Empire is in danger' and as Germany was the only country which is building a large fleet, Germany was pointed out as the quarter from which that danger threatened.[22]

Hyndman's defence once again involved trying to use anti-foreigner feelings to isolate his opponents (a strategy which was also adopted by *The Times* and other Tory papers).[23] Accusations of 'socialist jingoism' were levelled against Hyndman and the editor of *Justice*, leading to an acrimonious exchange between the two sides. Criticism of Hyndman reached a crescendo in 1909, culminating in a resolution from Rothstein's own branch, Central Hackney, urging the SDP executive to dissociate the party from his statements.[24] A number of letters supporting the Central Hackney branch were printed in *Justice* the following week, forcing the executive to moderate its line.

The following year Hyndman wrote a series of articles in the *Morning Post* accusing Germany of preparing for war with Britain and the debate erupted again.[25] It continued more or less continuously through to the outbreak of war. The old guard on the executive were only able to stave off further defeats at annual conferences at the expense of an increasingly bitter and divided party. But the growth of opposition to Hyndman threatened the right's control of the Party, and when H.W. Lee, party secretary for thirty years resigned in 1913, he was replaced by Albert Inkpin, a member of the Central Hackney branch who had been appointed Lee's deputy seven years earlier. He, along with his brother Harry and Rothstein's sister-in-law, Zelda Kahan, had been instrumental in drawing up the Central Hackney resolution condemning Hyndman's anti-German bias.

Walter Kendall rightly argued that this opposition developed further during the war years and provided most of the membership of the Communist Party. He saw the development of this opposition as evidence of the existence of a left-wing group in the British socialist movement capable of shrugging off the sectarian isolation of it past. Kendall was also correct to identify the anti-war movement as being 'forged in the pre-war years'.[26] But in order to emphasise the role of the Comintern in diverting that left along a different course, he ignores, or at best understates, the part played by Rothstein from August 1914 to October 1917.

War and the War Office

On the outbreak of war Rothstein resigned from the BSP, giving as his reasons the BSP's War Manifesto and support for the government's recruitment campaign. However, in the circumstances of the time when Russian political emigres were being threatened with internment under the Defence of the Realm Act (DORA), Rothstein found it expedient to resign from the party. Early on in the war—the precise date is difficult to establish—Rothstein secured his position in British society by volunteering for newspaper work in the War Office (WO). The exact nature of this work is difficult to establish, and significant controversy, therefore, surrounds these years. Morton and Tate in their history of *The British Labour Movement, 1770–1920* (1956) suggest that Rothstein, on resigning from the BSP, began immediate steps to bring together a few close associates—H.W. and Albert Inkpin, E.C. Fairchild and Joe Fineberg—in a determined struggle to end Hyndman's control of the BSP national executive and party organ *Justice*.[27] This claim was repeated by the Soviet historian N.A. Erofeev, and Rothstein's son Andrew, in *Imperializm i borba rabochego klassa* (*Imperialism and the Struggle of the Working Class*). None of these writers, however, mentioned Theodore Rothstein's work in the WO with M.I.7(d). Moreover, Andrew Rothstein has played down this employment by suggesting that his father was employed by Watergate House and not the WO, following a request from C.P. Scott who had been asked to recommend suitable people from the staff of the *Manchester Guardian*.[28]

Other writers have been more critical. Raymond Challinor, in his work on the Socialist Labour Party (SLP), has portrayed Rothstein as enjoying a comfortable position during the war while other Russian political emigres were either interned or deported. He repeats claims, made by Sylvia Pankhurst and J.T. Walton-Newbold, that Rothstein acted as confidential adviser to Lord Balfour on Russian affairs; and writes in support of Kendall's contention, taken uncritically from John Maclean, that Rothstein was a 'British agent'.[29]

John Saville has replied to these accusations in which he draws on a Foreign Office document produced by Rex Leeper to show that Rothstein's underground activities were not known to M.I.7(d). It becomes clear from this document that Rothstein had struck up a close friendship with Leeper. It was Leeper who was confidential adviser to Lord Balfour (the possible source of Walton-Newbold and Sylvia Pankhurst's suspicions). This memo, drawn up by the Foreign Office when the Home Office was calling for his deportation described Rothstein as an important contributor to the bulletin produced by the War Office, the *Daily Review of the Foreign Press (DRFP)*.[30]

Rothstein's employment by M.I.7(d) was useful in protecting him from anti-foreigner agitation and enabling him to earn a living. It also gave him access to foreign socialist materials and meant that he was able to play a secret but important role in channelling information to the socialist movement.[31] This employment also gave him access to Foreign Office officials and after 1917 helped to establish early relations between the British Government and the Bolshevik regime.

Peter Petrov and John Maclean

From 1914 until his deportation in September 1920 Rothstein continued to write for the socialist press under the pseudonyms John Bryan and WAMM.[32] During this period, contrary to the arguments put forward by Kendall and Challinor, Rothstein moved further away from those in the Russian political emigre community, who, owing to their lack of experience in the British labour movement, were dismissive of the internationalist opposition developing in both the BSP and the ILP. The arrest of Peter Petrov (a refugee from the 1905 Revolution and a close associate of John Maclean) in Glasgow under the Defence of the Realm Act on 22 December 1915 led to a disagreement between Petrov, Maclean and their supporters in Scotland on the one hand, and Rothstein and the London-based internationalists in the Central Hackney branch on the other. It was never properly healed. Maclean's suspicions of Rothstein, which led to his refusal of a full-time post with 'Hands Off Russia' in 1919, and, arguably, to his rejection of Communist Party membership, stemmed from earlier rivalries within the Russian political emigre community.

Peter Petrov's arrest, in the middle of Lloyd George's visit to the Clyde, led Petrov to suspect Rothstein's involvement in the campaign against him. In a letter written on 16 January 1916 to another prominent émigré, Georgii Chicherin (the future People's Commissar for Foreign Affairs), Petrov claimed Rothstein was untrustworthy:

> By the way, Rothstein was never connected with the movement. He was only connected with the dirty clique ... Rothstein always supported the Hyndman clique against the Marxist trend in Great Britain.[33]

Such accusations have to be seen in the circumstances surrounding Petrov's arrest. Petrov, who had been invited to Glasgow by John Maclean following the latter's arrest for a speech prejudicial to recruiting, was to act as a 'second organiser' for the party. However, Maclean and Petrov (along with Chicherin) had a wider agenda. They hoped to use the recent strike wave in Glasgow to gain support for the Zimmerwald Manifesto. They faced opposition not only in Glasgow and London, but also from London's Russian political emigre community led by Rothstein and Maxim Litvinov (Chicherin's future deputy in Narkomindel). The campaign to win support for the Zimmerwald Manifesto, which had called upon internationalists to break with all non-internationalists, had been taken up by Trotsky's Paris-based newspaper, *Nashe Slovo* (*Our Word*), and encouraged in Britain by Petrov and Chicherin. Rothstein, on the other hand opposed Zimmerwald, writing in *Nashe Slovo* that it was too early for such a split.[34] Opposition also came from the Clyde Workers' Committee (CWC) who were divided over the issue of the war, and the London-based internationalists within the BSP who called for the International Socialist Bureau (ISB) to be reconvened.

When, therefore, an article appeared in *Justice* the day after Petrov's arrest entitled 'Who and What is Peter Petrov?', many socialists expressed their fears that this article would further encourage the authorities on the Clyde to investigate Petrov's activities. It was in this climate of suspicion that Petrov voiced not only his misgivings concerning Rothstein, but also censured the entire national executive of the BSP for the campaign set against him. In the context of his impending trial when, according to William Gallacher and others, he saw police spies everywhere, Petrov hit out at those around him.[35] According to Andrew Rothstein, in a letter to David Burke, Petrov had visited Rothstein 'more than once, before and during the war ... at the latter's home (often I was present)'.[36] He must have been aware of Rothstein's activities before 1914.

In a further letter, Andrew Rothstein suggested that Petrov's attack on Rothstein and the NEC was in all likelihood determined by his close association with Maclean and his lieutenant James McDougall. At this juncture, the internationalist opposition to Hyndman was split between the Scottish advocates of Zimmerwald, and the London supporters of a reformed Second International. Petrov's suspicions of Rothstein reflected this divide. Andrew Rothstein's comments, on the other hand, provide some insight into the persistence of CPGB differences with Maclean and other Scottish critics of the British Communist Party:

The letter from Petrov to Chicherin makes funny reading. Petrov, reaching this country in 1907, would in any case have been too late to know of TR's 'connection with the movement' as a member of the SDF EC from 1901 to 1906, after openly attacking Hyndman over the Boer War issue in 1901. And he obviously knew nothing even as late as the last pre-war years, when TR was inspiring Zelda Coates, Fairchild and others to fight Hyndman's jingoism! ... That Petrov wrote this sort of thing in 1916, when he had made common cause with Maclean and Mc Dougall, is not surprising.[37]

BSP split

Rothstein's position on the war and the question of socialist policy, therefore, had placed him in sharp opposition to the more recent Russian emigres—Chicherin and Petrov—over the political situation created by the war. In particular whether Scotland was (in John Maclean's memorable phrase) 'in the rapids of revolution'; and over the question of whether anti-war socialists should support the Zimmerwald declaration and decisively break with the Second International. Rothstein and his colleagues remained reluctant to split the BSP until they felt confident that they had won over all the potential support. The split finally took place at the Easter 1916 conference, but Rothstein and his supporters in the Central Hackney branch were subject to fresh accusations in *Nashe Slovo*, and by Lenin in *Sotzial-Democrat*, that they shared many of the political assumptions of the old EC and 'the London gang'.[38] The controversy clearly showed Rothstein's deep political roots in the British movement and his distance from the Russian and continental opposition, until he shifted his ground to support the Zimmerwaldians just before the 1916 conference. Even so, the internationalist majority of the BSP continued to support moves to bring together all socialists in the belligerent countries and it was not until two years after October 1917 that the differences between Rothstein (and a majority of the BSP) and Fairchild began to move towards an open split.[39]

Rothstein's influence

Critics of Rothstein's influence on the British labour movement post-October 1917 have suggested that a native British revolutionary tradition was destroyed by the Comintern. The most virulent of these critics, Walter Kendall, has identified in the personalities of E.C. Fairchild and John Maclean both a reformist and a revolutionary challenge to British capitalism. The position of both men, he argued, was undermined by Rothstein's status as the embodiment of the Russian Revolution in Britain: a position strengthened by his role in distributing 'Moscow Gold' to compliant individuals and organisations. Kendall, however, largely misunderstood the effects of the events of 1917–20 on the political development of many British socialists. He failed to see that Fairchild, an ally of Rothstein's on most issues until 1919, shifted his ground in response to those members of the left (including many in the BSP) who were arguing for the new form of Soviet democracy. Maintaining his belief in Parliament as the appropriate means of working-class advance in Britain, Fairchild had set himself apart from those who rejected the Labour Party as the vehicle for socialism in Britain. It was this growing gulf that brought about his retirement from the BSP in 1919, not money from Moscow channelled through Rothstein.[40]

Maclean, on the other hand, was a marginalised figure on the British left by the end of 1919 owing to his long periods of imprisonment, and his deteriorating mental health. The cause of the disagreement between Rothstein and Maclean—an offer of a full-time post in 'Hands Off Russia'—was not intended to keep him from playing a full role in the unity negotiations, as Maclean maintained, but to bring him more securely into the fold. Maclean was very badly off, physically as well as financially, when he came out of prison. That Maclean came out with persecution mania was well known (a possible legacy from his dealings with Petrov?); to offer him a post in the 'Hands Off Russia' campaign was not an attempt to 'neutralise' him, any more than others were 'neutralised' by such activity.[41]

Turning Kendall on his head, Ray Challinor tried to show in his account of the SLP that Rothstein's influence on British socialist politics resulted in the 'reformist' elements of the BSP dominating the process of the debate and re-alignment that led from 1917 to the formation of the CPGB. In order to support this argument, Challinor attempts to show the political unreliability of Rothstein and the BSP's executive committee during the February Revolution. However, as John Saville has pointed out in his introduction to Rothstein's *From Chartism to Labourism*, Challinor's case is weakened by a selective misrepresentation of Rothstein's views on the entry of reformist ministers into the Provisional Government:

> The relevant quotation from Challinor reads: He (Rothstein) backed the entry of the Mensheviks into the Provisional Government, describing it as 'a great step which marked the official triumph of the revolutionary proletariat'. By contrast, he criticised the 'violent opposition of the Leninites'. It may be noted that the first two quotations from Rothstein are given in the reverse order in which they appeared in this *Plebs* article: a juxtaposition which imposes a somewhat different reading from that

which may have been intended. But what is inexcusable is that in the original there is no full stop after 'revolutionary proletariat' and the sentence continues with the words, 'but at the same time weakened its opposition to the bourgeoisie'. And later, in the same paragraph, Rothstein went on to illustrate 'How weak the position of the Socialist Ministers really is ....'[42]

Saville refers to Rothstein's final paragraph, which he quotes in full, as evidence of Rothstein's 'very good political sense, and independence of approach' in his political writings. Here Rothstein drew attention to the growing strength of the 'Jacobins (Bolsheviks)' and predicted that if the Provisional Government failed to deal with the worsening economic, political and military situation then it would pave the way for the Jacobins to assume power. The challenge of the Jacobins was an indication that the 'struggle of classes' had become 'the main factor in the Russian situation' and that the class struggle alone would determine the 'logical' outcome of the revolution. The revolution if it was to survive had to 'proceed to the next ascending phase of development.'[43]

However, Rothstein's role from 1918–20 as a representative of the Soviet Government and the Third International should not be underestimated. He operated in two crucial ways. First, he was instrumental in establishing contacts between the British Government and the Bolsheviks. He had contact with FO officials—notably Rex Leeper and Bruce Lockhart—whom he met regularly along with Litvinov, in cafés in London. Unofficial diplomatic relations were in fact established between the two countries 'over the luncheon table at a Lyons shop in the Strand' on 11 January 1918. Lockhart described the meeting between the four men with characteristic good humour:

> As we were ordering a sweet, Litvinoff noticed on the menu the magic words: 'pouding diplomate'. The idea appealed to him. The new diplomatist would eat the diplomatic pudding. The Lyons 'Nippy' took his order and returned a minute later to say there was no more. Litvinoff shrugged his shoulders and smiled blandly. 'Not recognised even by Lyons,' he said.[44]

Second, Rothstein did act as a channel for Russian funds to a variety of organisations and papers which either supported the Russian Revolution and Third International line on world revolution; or opposed the British Coalition government's policies of military intervention and economic isolation of the Soviet Union. These 'subventions' must, however, be seen in their proper context. Kendall, by combing the Cabinet reports on revolutionary organisations in Britain, has shown that through Rothstein the left groups received a total over two years of perhaps £15,000. The *Daily Herald* almost certainly received more from the Soviets than the left groups combined. The war of intervention, on the other hand, according to Lloyd George's own estimation in a speech delivered at the Guildhall on 8 November 1919, cost Britain £100 million.[45]

His activities as 'Moscow's paymaster' led to demands from some elements of the state and Government for his deportation, but his usefulness as a channel of communication led the F.O. Russian specialists Leeper and E.H. Carr (and Lloyd George acting on their advice) to resist expulsion pressures until Rothstein's ill-advised decision to visit Moscow in September 1920.[46]

But Rothstein's influence on the process of re-alignment on the left which led to the formation of the CPGB very clearly derived mainly from his long participation in, and considerable status within, the BSP and the left in general. Along with the majority of the BSP he had come to recognize (what Pankhurst and a few others had realised in late 1917–early 1918) that the October Revolution represented a clear and irrevocable break with the politics of reformism. However as the revolutionary wave dissipated in 1919–20, Rothstein's position came increasingly to coincide with that of the Bolshevik leadership. The increasing caution of Lenin's approach as shown in *Left Wing Communism* fitted in well with Rothstein's habits of political activity and thought developed over two and a half decades of politics on the British left. The Communist Party as it was formed in 1920 was very much in the mould of the BSP, with its essentially propagandist mode of activity. Not until the "Bolshevisation" policy was adopted in 1922 did the more agitational orientation and industrial orientation of some of the working-class cadres from the SLP come to prominence in the leadership of the Party.[47]

Postscript

By way of a short postscript: on his return to Moscow Rothstein was nominated Soviet Ambassador to Teheran. He was recalled in 1922 to assume a higher position in the commissariat of foreign affairs alongside Chicherin and Litvinov. In 1925 he was press director for the commissariat and also wrote for the Comintern press under the name Iranski. Between 1924 and 1925 he headed the World Economic and Political Institute. He was spared during the purges and in 1937 was elected a member of the Soviet Academy of Science. He died in 1953.[48]

David Burke and Fred Lindop teach at the University of Greenwich

Notes

1. Henry Pelling, *The British Communist Party: A Historical Profile* (Black,1958), p.191.
2. Walter Kendall, *The Revolutionary Movement in Britain 1900–1921* (Weidenfeld & Nicolson, 1969), p.xii.
3. For the Iskra period see V.I. Lenin, *Biograficheskaya Khronika, Tom 1 1870–1905 (Biographical Chronicle*, Vol.1) (Moscow, 1970), p.388 and I.M. Maiskii, 'Vstrechi s F.A. Rotshteinom v Dorevolyutsionnie Vremena' in *Imperializm i borba rabochego klassa* (Moscow, 1960), pp.56–8. ('Meetings with Th. Rothstein in pre-revolutionary times' in *Imperialism and the Struggle of the Working-Class*.) For the Russian Trading Delegation see Kendall, *Revolutionary Movement*, p.238 and fn.14 p.402. Also FO371/6399, 12 January 1921.
4. Martin Crick, *The History of the Social Democratic Federation* (Ryburn Publishing, Keele University Press, 1994).
5. Ibid., p.285.
6. 'David Burke, 'Theodore Rothstein, Russian Emigré and British Socialist', in John Slatter (ed.), *From the Other Shore: Russian Political Emigrants in Britain, 1880–1917* (1984), pp.81–100.
7. Andrew Rothstein, 'The Revolutionary Movement in Britain, 1900–1921', *Labour Monthly*, Dec.1969, p.567.
8. Biographical material taken from David Burke's correspondence with Andrew Rothstein 1980–91, and from *Imperializm* pp.5–6.
9. See N.A. Erofeev and I.M. Maiskii in *Imperializm* pp. 10 and 55 respectively. Also W.P. Crozier to C.P Scott letter dated 1 May 1911 (sic), C.P. Scott Papers A/R58/1. John Ryland's University Library of Manchester; and Andrew Rothstein letter to D. Burke dated 20 August 1991: 'My reference to my father's work is correct. He went to Fleet Street—first the *Daily News* and then the *Guardian*—in the evenings. Papers were smaller then. He was a fully-fledged member of the NUJ. His post was that of a special correspondent, dealing with foreign news (but not as a foreign editor).'
10. *Justice*, 3 October 1896.
11. *Social-Democrat*, March 1898.
12. *Justice*, 18 December 1898.
13. Ibid., 7 April 1900.
14. *Social-Democrat*, June 1900.
15. *Justice*, 21 September 1901.
16. *Justice*, 30 August 1902.
17. Ibid., 7 March 1903.
18. Ibid., 9 March 1907.
19. Ibid., 18 August 1906.
20. Ibid., 27 January 1906.
21. Ibid.
22. Ibid., 3 April 1909.
23. Ibid., see *The Times*, esp. 29 March–3 April 1909.

24. *Justice*, 30 July 1910.
25. *Morning Post*, 6 July 1910.
26. Kendall, *Revolutionary Movement*, p.61.
27. E.C. Fairchild. 1874–1953. Joined ILP in 1894, SDF in 1895. Full-time SDF organiser 1910–12. Continuously member of SDF Executive from 1909 to 1917 with only one year's gap in 1913. A leading figure in the pre-war opposition to Hyndman. See Kendall *Revolutionary Movement*, p.327, fn36. Joe Fineberg. 1886–1957. Born at Zhoklin, Russian Poland, he was brought to England by his parents in 1888. Became secretary of the Stepney & Whitechapel branch of the SDF. Elected to the executive of the BSP in 1914. Re-elected 1915, 1916 and 1917. After the October Revolution he acted as a secretary to Litvinov, who was appointed Soviet Ambassador to Britain on 3 January 1918. In June 1918, however, Fineberg returned to Russia and, once there, his experience abroad was utilised in setting up the Communist International. 1925–26 Tass correspondent in Peking. Later he worked in the Foreign Languages Publishing House and, among other things, translated into English *Days and Nights*, Konstantin Simonov's war novel on Stalingrad. See Kendall Revolutionary Movement, fn.48, p.328, and *Vospominania o V.I. Lenine (Memories of Lenin)*, Vol.3, Moscow 1960, pp.205–9 and 383; A.L. Morton and George Tate, *The British Labour Movement* (Lawrence and Wishart, 1956), p.258.
28. Andrew Rothstein, letter to D. Burke, 13 January 1981.
29. Raymond Challinor, *The Origins of British Bolshevism* (Croom Helm, 1977), pp.246–7; Kendall Revolutionary Movement, p.247 fn.16.
30. Theodore Rothstein, *From Chartism to Labourism: Historical Sketches of the English working-class Movement* (Lawrence and Wishart: 1983), Introduction by John Saville, p.xv. See also FO 371/347/17951, 29 October 1918.
31. 'By gaining a far wider access to foreign press opinions and events abroad than he had ever had before my father was in a position to inform his anti-war work.' Andrew Rothstein letter to David Burke, 13 January 1981.
32. 'So who were these initials? Mozart! Father passionately loved classical German music.' Andrew Rothstein, *Imperializm*, p.51.
33. Petrov to Chicherin, letter post-marked 24 January 1916, Bridges Adams Papers cited Ron Grant, 'G.V. Chicherin and the Russian Revolutionary Cause in Great Britain', in John Slatter (ed.) *From the Other Shore*, 1984, p.123.
34. See *Nashe Slovo*, 7 December 1915.
35. See *Justice*, 23 December 1915, 20 & 27 January 1916. Also William Gallacher, *Revolt on the Clyde: An Autobiography* (Lawrence and Wishart, 1936), pp.59–62; Harry McShane and Joan Smith, *No Mean Fighter*, 1978, pp.77–8; Nan Milton, John Maclean (Pluto: 1973), pp.108–12.
36. Andrew Rothstein, letter to D. Burke 15 August 1982.
37. Ibid., letter dated 27 August 1982.
38. Lenin, 'Split or Decay', Written between February/April 1916 but not published until 1931. *Collected Works,* 4th edn. Vol.xxii, Moscow 1964, p.180. See also *Nashe Slovo*, 11 July and 8 August 1916.

39. For the debate between Fairchild and supporters of Sovietism see *The Call*, 17 and 24 April 1916.
40. John Maclean 'Open Letter to Lenin', *The Socialist*, 3 February 1921.
41. The most obvious example is Harry Pollitt; others include J.T. Walton-Newbold, Zelda Kahan and W.P. Coates.
42. Saville, introduction to Rothstein, *From Chartism to Labourism*, pp.xiii–xiv.
43. Ibid., p.xiv; John Bryan (Theodore Rothstein), 'The Struggle of Classes in Russia', *Plebs Magazine*, August 1917, p.147.
44. R.H. Bruce Lockhart, *Memoirs of a British Agent* (Macmillan, 1974), p.204.
45. Cabinet Papers (CAB 24) from 1920 onwards draw attention to Rothstein financing several left-wing groups, and paying money to individuals. Most of these sums were small, apart from the subsidy to the *Daily Herald* whose overtures to the Russian Trade Delegation for funds were, in fact, initially rejected. The BSP had (in the two years before the CPGB was established) some £3,000 or more; Sylvia Pankhurst's WSF no less; the SLP in 1919 'nearly £300'; the People's Russian Information Bureau, which circulated facts and documents from Soviet Russia in 1918–20, about £1,000; the shop stewards' movement 'a considerable subsidy' (put by one ex-Communist at £4000). See also CAB 24/111/1804.
46. FO 371/3347/179551, 29 October 1918.
47. See Richard Hyman and James Hinton, *Trade Unions and Revolution: The Industrial Politics of the Early British Communist Party* (Pluto, 1975), p.17.
48. That he was spared in the purges seems all the more remarkable given the claim made by Francis Beckett in *The Enemy Within: The Rise and Fall of the British Communist Party* (John Murray, 1995) that Andrew Rothstein found 'himself in a Soviet prison and hours away from execution'. See also Kevin Morgan's comments in a review of Beckett, in *Labour History Review*, volume 60.3 (Winter 1995), p.60. In connection with the Rothsteins' activities in the Soviet Union see 'A Note on the Rothstein Family', FO371/2952/65655.

Socialist History: A personal note
Willie Thompson

During the greater part of the existence of the CP Historians (after 1957 simply History Group), its regular publication was the pamphlet-format *Our History*, a single-authored account or analysis exploring one particular theme. In all, over forty of these were produced, most of them reaching a very high standard of information and interpretation. In the late seventies the Group attempted to supplement this with a slighter publication carrying shorter pieces and discussion items. It was aimed principally at internal circulation and was given the title *Our History Journal*.

Initially, after an optimistic beginning, the project was not a success. For although what was produced was both stimulating and enlightening, the economic reality of the time acted against this printed and (given the Group's resources) quite lavishly produced journal and the costs could not be sustained. In 1982–3 therefore, I was asked by John Attfield, the then Secretary of the Group, to restart the *OHJ* on the basis of a publication of up to twenty A4 pages produced by means of what was even then fairly obsolescent technology—cyclostyled stencils.

At the beginning it was a fairly simple operation, made easier by considerable assistance from Bill Moore, who became the Group's Secretary. Given the space at our disposal the pieces were necessarily short and the quality of production, though as good as the circumstances permitted, necessarily rather basic. It was the period of great turmoil within the Communist Party, leading to its disbandment and *OHJ* reflected this development, though I tried to avoid allowing the journal to be dominated by current controversies and becoming simply a forum for polemical interpretations of the CP's history. However, I did believe it was important to base ourselves upon historical honesty and to look the past in the face, and therefore adopted a deliberate policy of discussing episodes in the history of the communist movement, in Britain and internationally, where it had behaved in a discreditable or even odious fashion. This naturally provoked controversy, and in my view that was to the benefit of both *OHJ* and the History Group.

In the late 1980s further developments in information technology brought onto the scene personal computers which were capable of imitating the printed page, and therefore opened the possibility of desktop publishing. After eight numbers our cyclostyled *OHJ*, which had served us well for five years, was consigned to final retirement, the journal adopted a format similar to that of *Our History*, and now looked more like a proper magazine, with 50–60 pages of A5 size. The new technology made this economically feasible. It also meant however that since the journal was printed directly from the pages prepared by the editor (and also it was bigger), a lot more work was required typing, formatting and checking the copy.

The redesigned journal now also tried to reach beyond the boundaries of the Group and find a wider sale; however it continued with its old title, and this was capable of giving rise to considerable confusion among potential buyers on account of the similarity with *Our History*. I recall an occasion when quite accidentally I was in Central Books and saw the assistant and a customer became hopelessly entangled because of a mutual misunderstanding about the respective titles. Happily on this occasion I was able to resolve it for them, but there must have been many similar incidents, and for this reason among others the title was changed to *Socialist History Journal* in 1992.

That date gives a clue as to the other important reason for the alteration. At the end of 1991 the Communist Party disbanded and was reincarnated as Democratic Left, a wholly different sort of political formation. The position of a CP History Group in these circumstances (where full membership was restricted to Party members) was clearly anomalous, and so that too transformed itself—into the Socialist History Society, with membership open to everybody (though remaining affiliated to Democratic Left).

By that time however a more far-reaching change was in prospect. The opportunity appeared of having the *SHJ* printed and distributed by a commercial publisher—though one identified with the left—in this case Pluto Press. After a certain amount of heart-searching, the Society decided to pursue this option, and a number of important changes followed. It was concluded that it would not be practicable to maintain both *Our History* and OHJ, and since the new situation permitted considerably longer articles to appear in the journal, the decision was taken that the two publications should be amalgamated under the title *Socialist History*. Thus the *Our History* series came to an end, although the occasional papers produced by the Society carry on the tradition to some extent.

A further development was the fact that each issue of *Socialist History*, unlike its predecessors, was henceforth to be focused upon (though not exclusively devoted to) a particular theme. With the adoption of more professional publication arrangements an editorial team was formed, which shared the burden of editorial work, along with an advisory group of distinguished historians. These innovations contributed to the establishment of longer-term planning of editorial content and thereby gave direction to the journal's development.

The arrangement worked successfully and at three numbers per year, six issues were produced in this manner before it was decided to go over to a scheme of two issues per year but with an enlarged number of pages, providing overall more content. Six further numbers were published up to the end of 1997, but then Pluto found itself unable to continue with the arrangement. As a consequence only one number appeared in the course of 1998, and this was with the publisher which has taken over the production and distribution of *Socialist History*, Rivers Oram. Clearly some time was required to establish new arrangements. We are expecting to catch up with the gap in the course of 1999, when for that occasion only, three issues will be published. For success in negotiating the transition we have to thank particularly Mike Waite, Steve Woodhams, Francis King and David Morgan.

It is at this point that I will be standing down as editor, a change which has been in preparation over the past year. It has always been my opinion that a single individual should not remain for too lengthy a period in such responsibilities, and in my own case this has now extended to 17 years. I have to say that for my own part it has been an enormously rewarding and stimulating experience (though naturally not without its share of difficulties and crises), and I would not wish to have missed it for anything. Working with fellow-editors, advisors, authors, publishers and the committee of the Society had been profoundly educative as well as enjoyable. It's appropriate to note, since Mike Waite is also in the process of standing down as reviews editor, that the journal's success has been due in great part to his work in that capacity, in selection of books and reviewers and seeing that the reviews get written—as well as helping to determine *SH*'s general direction. The result has been a reviews section that would be the envy of many a well-established journal of much greater circulation.

It is an index of the strength of any institution, especially small ones with limited resources, that its leading personnel can change at a point of successful development so that it becomes further strengthened and more able to fulfil its role. I'm convinced as firmly as anybody can be that under its new editor and expanded editorial team *Socialist History* is going to advance in circulation, in impact and in standing and indeed become a leading journal of its kind for the twenty-first century.

Willie Thompson

Reviews

Nineteenth-century millennium

Edward Royle, *Robert Owen and the Commencement of the Millennium. A Study of the Harmony Community* (Manchester University Press, 1998), ISBN 0 71905 426 5, xi + 274 pp., £45.00 hbk.

The Harmony, or Queenwood, community in Hampshire, founded by Robert Owen's followers in 1839, represented the apogee of early socialist efforts in Britain. It was not only much the most focused attempt to found a rural community where unemployed urban labourers could be relocated, dwarfing experiments at Orbiston, Manea Fen, and elsewhere in Britain, and occupying some six years of the most influential period of Owen's career until its collapse in 1845. The community was also intended symbolically to represent the extension of the highest possible standard of living in the 'old, immoral world' of capitalism to the working classes in the new. No expense was spared, no attention to detail regarded as insignificant where lavishing funds on the main Queenwood building was concerned: this was to be a palace, or country house, on the grandest scale. As George Jacob Holyoake, a sometime Owen lieutenant gaoled for blasphemy, and visitor to the community, observed, the building was 'built with the care that befitted a sacred edifice. The parts out of sight were finished as scrupulously as those that met the eye', even the nails furthest removed from public vision being of the highest quality. The kitchen, famously, had a mechanical system of dumb-waiters for serving and clearing dishes which was well in advance of any other in the country. Basement rooms were lined with mahogany, and seven or eight hundred pounds expended in laying out roads and gardens on the estate. The building was a work of art; 'beauty had no terrors for them', Holyoake added, defending the early socialists from any accusations of philistinism. The 'C. M.', or

'Commencement of the Millennium' stone laid in 1839 summed up the expectations of socialists everywhere. Eventually, they hoped, the entire society was to be relocated, and 'Community' would become the model of social organisation, with (in Owen's most measured plans, published in *The Book of the New Moral World*, 1836–44), society superseding the old, harmful system of the division of labour by being re-divided into age-groups, whereby each person would pass through stages of education, employment, supervision and education of others, and management of the community and its relations with other communities.

Folly

But Queenwood proved to be folly on the grandest scale. Owen had a reputation derived from his New Lanark days, some twenty years earlier, of astute managerial and financial expertise. But his own fortune had been long since expended, mostly at New Harmony in Indiana. He found a few sympathetic, wealthy backers for Queenwood, and the Socialist movement (the upper case use being common from the mid-1830s) organised in some fifty branches, chiefly in the midlands, with at least ten thousand visitors to Sunday lectures, dances and soirées, contributed a steady flow of funds. But Owen himself, who turned seventy in 1841, had long since allowed the grandiosity of his visions to overtake any youthful practicality. He had gambled at New Lanark, often on an enormous scale, paying far more than the establishment was worth to out-vie wayward partners and gain control over the mills. He had always won there, but was rarely to enjoy fortune thereafter. The gamble at Queenwood was that an established community would lure thousands to similar colonies on the land, thus outstripping competition from the Chartists (who under Feargus O'Connor began to devise a small-farm initiative of their own, which proved no more successful). The chief risk in the first instance was that the five hundred acres of land, chosen quickly, would not prove sufficiently productive, or the location advantageous. But the chief difficulty which developed by 1840 was simply the enormous cost of the buildings. When over £30,000 had been sunk into the estate, funds dried up. The collapse was rapid and total, and with Queenwood the entire early Socialist movement sank. Never again would the model community serve as the ideal form of socialist society on any appreciable scale. Marx, and even more Engels, enthusiasts to a degree while the community thrived, quickly opted for a national system based upon state centralisation, an idea Owen rejected. For a generation, until the name of Owen was virtually forgotten outside of the co-operative movement, there was little socialism to speak of in Britain. The 'Harmony Hall' building was destroyed by fire in 1902, having been a school for half a century, and the experiment virtually disappeared from memory thereafter.

Owen's outlook

As a noted social historian Edward Royle explores this grand experiment in a characteristically thorough and impressive fashion. Having worked on Owen and the secularist movement some twenty-five years ago, he brings the requisite expertise, and persuades us that while much is known of New Harmony, it is anomalous to have neglected Queenwood, whose national significance is equally impressive, for so long. Royle commences with a general overview of Owen's early life and education, his career at New Lanark, and the development of the 'new views', as Owen called them after his *A New View of Society* (1813) appeared. The 'views', of course, were not very new, particularly until 1817, when Owen's combination of them added communal living and economic organisation to his nostrums for poor relief to his early (and always deep-seated) paternalist proposals for better supervision, infant education, and a safer, cleaner, more just workplace and living environment. This communal step went appreciably beyond the New Lanark experience, and combined with Owen's attacks on organised religion and political economy (both thriving at this point) resulted in Owen increasingly distancing himself from both well-wishers and critics alike, and focusing his efforts on the acquisition and development of New Harmony in the mid-1820s.

Royle's second chapter examines the development of the co-operative and communitarian movement from the early 1820s until 1837, and the emergence of organised Owenism in the mid-1830s, and helps to contextualise Owenism by setting it beside the Spencean movement, Christian Socialism, the Chartist Land Plan and similar efforts to relocate the working classes to a rural environment. With chapter three commences the close analysis of the Harmony community proper. Royle's strength here is not most obviously, and merely, in the provision of a wealth of detail about the community itself, and about the linkage between the branches (about which surprisingly little research has been done) and efforts to construct the community. Royle analyses the abortive negotiations to acquire communities at Wisbech and Manea Fen, which in retrospect look like more attractive options, for early scrutiny of the soil at Queenwood concluded that it was prone to drought, with poor soil and a chalky base which drained rainfall rapidly, no rivers or streams, poor communication with the outside world, and in need of extensive capital investment. Royle suggests that 'this should have been conclusive' (78) and the estate rejected. Despite many warnings, Owen proceeded. Gradually, from pessimism in the summer of 1839, socialists warmed to the purchase, and began to focus their eventual hopes on relocating there (while employing much of their surplus capital in building branch halls for more immediate purposes, which, as Royle indicates, may have directly undermined the community at a critical point.) Building began in earnest at the end of 1839, with some 45 persons, including eight children, resident in a cramped farmhouse the first cold winter. The first recruits were ruled with an iron hand by the Liverpool Owenite John Finch, who was much concerned to enforce teetotalism on members. By mid-1841 many residents had left, some involved in construction being uninterested in agriculture, and only nineteen, including seven children, remained. It was scarcely the new moral world on the grand scale.

Owenite organisation

In chapter four, Royle retreats from this depressing picture to examine the wider branch movement upon which the community depended. He here addresses the vexed question of the religiosity of Owenism. Superficially—as his title indicates—Owenism was much indebted to various strands of early nineteenth century millennarianism, or at least to a language which expressed rapid social and moral change for the better. Beyond this, the organisation of the chief Owenite organisation of the late 1830s and early 1840s, the Association of All Classes of All Nations, owed much to the Methodist class system, terming their lecturers 'Social Missionaries' and engaging in extensive and prolonged theological debates with their orthodox opponents. Many individual Owenites also expressed fervent religious beliefs, though Owen himself, of course, and some leading followers like Holyoake, were deists, or even, like Charles Southwell, atheists. Owenism as a whole bears much affinity to Christian sectarianism, and its ultimate goals—enhanced sociability. benevolence, friendship and community—closely resemble the ideals of various sects, notably the Quakers, as well as, in broad outline, the notional aspirations of the religion as a whole. But if Owenism was never just another 'sect', its religiosity was an attractive element to many, just as its heterodoxy proved (as had been the case for Thomas Paine) crucial to undermining wider, and especially middle-class, public support.

Community life

On 30 August 1841 Owen laid the foundation stone for the new community and commenced the new millennium. Money flowed in rapidly, but 90 per cent was in the form of loans, economic distress having restricted branch contributions. By mid-1842 these totalled over £15,000, and it emerged that Owen was chiefly indebted to one man, Frederick Bate, rather than any philanthropic consortium. By mid-1843 some financial balance had been achieved, and by 1844 a peak of ninety members (36 being children, one of whom, the first born in the new community, was Primo Communist Flitcroft, 'a lovely child') had been reached. Most of these were working class, only a fifth of whom had agricultural experience. Their leaders, chiefly Charles Frederick Green, William Pare, John Finch and William Galpin, were mainly businessmen with a co-operative bent and a close identification (certainly in Finch's and Galpin's case) with the millennarian aspects of Owenism. Royle offers brief vignettes of their collective community life (for detail is scarce) which by and large seems to have been happy (the hired labourers could retire to neighbouring pub for beer), though there were complaints about food, lack of privacy (domestic officers could enter even married quarters) and the lack of self-government of the members. Despite Owen's ideals, women found themselves largely relegated to traditional roles. With heroic efforts, the land, eventually extended to over a thousand acres, proved more productive than some had anticipated, but the costs of hired labour proved exorbitant.

Education and leisure activities were well developed. Had funds been available the community might well have been a success. Had Owen's whimsicality and tenacious paternalism not soured Socialist politics, funds might have been available. But there was never enough time to new-form Socialist character. By late 1844 the branches were in open rebellion against Owen, but it was too late. The community closed on 29 September 1845, an act of folly, for Royle, but also 'a noble failure' (122). This is an admirably detailed study of a crucial moment in the early socialist movement. If the contents of the millennium dome were nearly as social as those envisaged by the Queenwood pioneers, it too might arouse enthusiasm.

Gregory Claeys
Royal Holloway, University of London

Religion, Labour and the New Jerusalem

Robert Pope, *Building Jerusalem: Nonconformity, Labour and the Social Question in Wales, 1906–1939* (University of Wales Press, Cardiff, 1998), xiv and 266pp., ISBN 0 708301 413 9, £25.00 hbk.

As we stand on the threshold of the millennium, both the urban and rural landscapes of Wales still bear eloquent witness to the influence of organised religion—and especially the influence of Nonconformity—upon the life of the country during the Victorian period. The thousands of chapels, which are such prominent features of the built environment, were the products of a remarkable explosion of religiosity: today only the vapour trails remain. Nonetheless, the shockwaves continued to reverberate well into the twentieth century, and whilst Welsh historians usually acknowledge this fact, they have been slow to produce histories which place organised religion at centre stage. As a consequence, any book that explicitly sets out to examine the place of the Free Churches in Wales during the early decades of the twentieth century is to be welcomed.

Building Jerusalem is an attempt to fill this significant historiographical gap. Written by Robert Pope, a theology lecturer, the book attempts to trace the history of a particular aspect of secularisation in Wales; namely, the impact of the labour movement upon the fortunes of the chapels. After opening with a chapter entitled 'Setting the scene', in which some of the more familiar developments in the history of both the labour movement and organised religion are rehearsed, Pope moves us into less well-known territory. A variety of Nonconformist thinkers are introduced to the reader, and their various responses to the burgeoning labour movement are discussed in some detail. Three main positions were adopted. Some within the chapels conceived of Socialism as a practical application of Christian principles. Others, not necessarily hostile to the labour movement, believed that Nonconformity still had its own unique contribution to make when it came to social questions. Finally, there were those who, almost from the outset, were simply antagonistic to socialism. These sections of the book, which sketch out the various theological arguments deployed in the early years of the century, are extremely illuminating. They serve as a useful reminder of the range of possibilities that existed at a time when it was by no means clear that the labour movement was about to make a decisive breakthrough in Wales, nor that Nonconformity was embarking upon a period of decline.

Pope goes on to identify an important turning point in the history of the Free Churches. As in so many other spheres of Welsh life, 1910–11 apparently marked something of a watershed. Just as the forces were unleashed which led to miners rioting on the streets of Tonypandy, opinion-makers in the chapels began to develop a new approach to the problems faced by the working class. This social conscience was articulated at the same time as a general withdrawal of Nonconformists from the political sphere, a move that Pope concludes did them 'more harm than good'. 'Labour' was becoming ever more politicised and the lost proletarian sheep were, he suggests, unlikely to be attracted back to the explicitly non-political chapels. The rest of the book considers some of the ways in which this new-found social conscience both manifested itself and then ultimately failed to effect the move to a more just society.

Building Jerusalem is an important contribution to the historiography but it is not without its shortcomings. There is a worrying declaration in the Preface that some quotations from primary sources have been amended to rid them of sexist language. No indication is given of which quotations have been tampered with, nor what the original versions contained. This is a sin that perhaps only theologians, and not historians, could commit. More profound is the failure to meet some of the goals that are set out in the opening pages of the book. Pope promises to consider the problematic relationship between labour and the chapels 'from both the workingclass and the Nonconformist point of view'. In fact, we hear a lot from the latter, and hardly anything from the former. This should not surprise. The sources that would enable him to capture 'what religious and political allegiance meant to the working class' are few and far between. However, readers should not be misled into thinking they are buying a social history of Nonconformity. Nor should they hope to find a treasure house of new insights into the history of the labour movement in Wales: this may be an examination of labour history from the perspective of the pulpit instead of the union lodge, but it locates itself securely in orthodox chronologies and understandings. Instead, the real achievement of Robert Pope lies in his recovery of the theological debates that raged within the chapels at a defining, and ultimately decisive, moment in their history.

Andy Croll
Andy Croll is a Lecturer in Modern British History
at the University of Glamorgan

Women's suffrage

Maroula Joannou and June Purvis (eds), *The Women's Suffrage Movement: New Feminist Perspectives* (Manchester University Press, Manchester, 1998), xii and 227pp., ISBN 0 7190 486 0, £45.00 hbk.

Although the fight for votes for women is often the only aspect of women's history which is taught in schools, too often this is presented as a single narrative largely untouched by revisionist scholarship. In recent years, the work of Sandra Holton, of June Hannam, and of Liz Stanley and Ann Morley, building in different ways on Jill Liddington and Jill Norris's *One Hand Tied Behind Us*, (1978), have de-centred the dominant narrative which focuses on London, the Edwardian period, the Pankhursts and the Women's Social and Political Union (WSPU). Their writing, taken with a wealth of material only slowly emerging from unpublished PhDs and a number of published and forthcoming collections, now amounts almost to a new orthodoxy, at least among suffrage historians. This provides, not surprisingly, a much more complex picture of a movement with strong roots into the nineteenth century in terms of personnel but also in terms of ideology and strategy.

It is no longer simply a story of two increasingly antipathetic strands, one of constitutionalism, the other of militancy. Individual women and men—for men too had a part to play as suffragists—moved between or held joint membership of organisations traditionally characterised as opposed and certainly 'militants' and 'constitutionalists' could work together productively at a local level. Provincial studies of suffragism have shown the importance of pre-existing as well as suffrage-based personal and political networks. Biographical work has added to these more nuanced accounts by placing particular suffragist women into a context where suffrage politics interacted with other politics; where individuals changed their minds about organisations, people and tactics; and where suffrage politics stretched across and beyond the first world war.

Joannou and Purvis have edited a volume which claims to be part of the reappraisal and rewriting of the history of the suffrage agitation. It certainly contributes to a resurgence of writing on suffrage history yet in many ways it is a rather curious collection. In particular the chapters on suffragism and culture sit rather awkwardly with the chapters that focus more on specific organisations. The fragmented nature of the collection is highlighted by the presence of a fine piece on the Women's Franchise League by Sandra Holton, as it is the only chapter concerned with the nineteenth century, and by Lesley Hall's isolated chapter on suffrage and sex reform. In short, the overall purpose of the volume, other than a broad brief of reclamation, is not very clear. If its audience is principally those who are reasonably literate in suffrage history, then one could ask how much this collection adds in terms of approach or the retrieval of unfamiliar empirical data. If, instead, the audience, is presumed to know little of suffrage history, then many of the pieces are too specific. Most importantly, does this collection fire the imagination of the novice student of suffrage history? The answer would have to be, it could in parts. For there are few connections made between chapters and the authors do not appear to have been asked to address a common agenda. In many ways, therefore, the chapters have to stand alone and suggest a volume to be dipped into rather than read as a whole. Many of the contributions, particularly those drawing attention to neglected organisations or issues, are frustratingly short. Only Holton is allowed the space to develop her argument in more detail.

There are also some curious omissions from the book as a whole. One significant aspect of the fight for women's enfranchisement, the demand for adult suffrage (that all women and men should qualify for the vote irrespective of property qualification), is not the subject of any of the fourteen studies which make up the volume. Indeed adult suffrage is barely mentioned, even in passing, by most of the contributing authors and, when it does appear, is stereotyped as a mask hiding antisuffragism. Yet significant numbers of individuals and much of the labour movement formulated their sincere demand for women's enfranchisement in these terms. Although Cheryl Law provides a useful, although rather brief, examination of the period from 1918 to 1928 asking whether universal suffrage was a legislative inevitability, the key period of transition in suffrage politics of the first world war is only touched upon by her. An aspect of suffrage politics during the war also finds some space in Krista Cowman's interesting contribution on the United Suffragists, but this is necessarily only part of the story. 1914 did not constitute the closure in suffrage politics that some of the authors imply.

Nevertheless this collection does draw attention to organisations about which relatively little has been published—the Women's Freedom League, Women's Tax Resistance League and the United Suffragists—as well as increasingly important issues to the new suffrage history, such as the provincial movement, class and suffragism as well as the continuing campaign for universal suffrage in the 1920s. A number of contributions are linked by an interest in exploring the meaning of militancy for different organisations and for individuals. Michelle Myall's portrait of Mary Leigh, a working-class suffragette, challenges a number of the prevalent assumptions about the

WSPU and their most active members. Myall explores the motivation of a woman whose militancy led to more than nine periods of imprisonment. Leigh was amongst the first to be force-fed in 1909 and Myall gives a clear picture of what militant action cost the perpetrator. Although rightly drawing attention to the participation of working-class women in the WSPU after the break with the Independent Labour Party (ILP) in 1907, there are other aspects of the class experience of WSPU members which are left unanswered: how did working-class women, like Leigh, survive economically during their militant years? What difference did Leigh's class make to her experience of the WSPU and how did she relate to other working-class WSPU activists like Jennie Baines? Did the attitudes of other WSPUers to working-class women change over the organisation's lifetime, and if so, why?

This is a collection which never really succeeds in drawing together its cultural and more historical foci. In two separate volumes, the authors might have had more space to develop their ideas, to make more explicit links with each other's arguments, and thus produce a more nuanced picture of the complexity of the suffrage movement from its roots in the nineteenth century to its final campaigns of the 1920s. That said, individual contributions provide useful introductions to neglected aspects of suffrage history and together suggest that there is still room for fruitful research in an area of women's history about which it is generally assumed that all that can be said, has been said.

Karen Hunt
Manchester Metropolitan University

Revolutionary encyclopaedia

Edward Acton, *Vladimir Iu. Cherniaev and William G. Rosenberg* (eds), *Critical Companion to the Russian Revolution 1914–1921* (Arnold, London, 1997), xviii and 782 pp., ISBN 0 340 61454 4, £59.95 hbk.

This substantial work is the product of fruitful international co-operation with joint-editors from Britain (Edward Acton), the USA (William Rosenberg) and Russia (Vladimir Cherniaev). It combines the reference function of an encyclopaedia with an interpretive treatment in its 67 entries by specialists who also probe questions awaiting further clarification. Twenty of its 46 contributors are from the USA and 14 from Britain; 8 are from Russia (mostly from St Petersburg) and are well translated.

Entries, mostly of 3,000–5,000 words, are grouped thematically in eight sections. 'The Revolution as Event' includes essays on Russia in World War 1, the February and October Revolutions, the Civil War and Foreign Intervention. The section on personalites comprises entries on two Bolsheviks (Lenin and Trotsky), two Mensheviks (Martov and Tsereteli), three Socialist Revolutionaries (Kerensky, Chernov and the Left S-R leader Spiridonova), one Constitutional Democrat (Miliukov), Tsar Nicholas II and the White Generals. References to other leaders can be located through a very useful index of names, prepared in Russia, giving dates and details of 500 personalities featured in the book. There is also a comprehensive index of subjects, and suggestions for further reading given after each entry, but unfortunately sources of quotations are not specified.

The main parties and movements from the Anarchists to the Constitutional Democrats have separate entries, and Robert V. Daniels writes additionally on 'The communist opposition'. He notes that 'a striking feature of the Russian Revolution was the persistence of political pluralism within the victorious Communist Party throughout the most violent and uncertain period of revolutionary struggle, the era of war communism between 1918 and 1921.'

Sixteen essays are grouped under the rubric of Institutions and Institutional Cultures. Along with entries on the Soviet State, the Cheka, the Press, and the Constituent Assembly there are essays on such themes as Education, Schools and Student Life; Family, Marriage and Relations between the Sexes; and the Russian Orthodox Church. Different aspects of peasant life are expertly treated in three essays by Orlando Figes. A section on Social Groups, Identities, Culture and Consciousness includes entries on the Intelligentsia, the Industrialists, Soldiers and Sailors, and Women and the Gender Question. In a wide-ranging treatment of the Workers, Sergei Iarov, of St Petersburg, assesses their numbers, composition, distribution, levels of skill, material conditions and unemployment figures. He argues that, although it did not realise the dictatorship of the proletariat as claimed, 'to a certain degree and in a peculiar way' the Soviet regime 'brought political administration within the reach of the workers'. This is a view not shared by William Rosenberg who in his introduction states categorically that '"proletarian dictatorship" very quickly became an uncompromising dictatorship over, not by, industrial and agrarian labour'. Two further sections contain essays on Economic Issues and Problems of Everyday Life, and on Nationality and Regional Questions.

Edward Acton contributes a hard-hitting polemical introduction on the Historiography of the Revolution. He shows how from the 1960s and early 1970s mainline Sovietology was called into question by a 'new wave' embracing a majority of Western specialists on the revolution. A fresh broadly conceived 'revisionist' approach began to view the period 'from below', challenging the cold war picture of a simple Russian people being manipulated and brainwashed by power-hungry Bolshevik intellectuals. Research was now directed to objective social processes. These were seen as providing the background against which the working people were radicalised and 'the complex amalgam which was Bolshevism came to "articulate" working-class aspirations.' Thus the October Revolution had a mass popular base and could not simply be reduced to a conspiratorial *coup d'état*.

Dogmas and nostrums

Meanwhile in the USSR in the late 1980s old official 'Marxist-Leninist' dogmas began to be increasingly subjected to critical scrutiny betokening a basis for a rapprochement with Western 'revisionist' historians. However the subsequent collapse of the Soviet Union led in Russia to a swing to the right with a wholesale adoption of the nostrums of traditional Western sovietology, which in the USA Richard Pipes took up the cudgels to reassert. Acton explains that a reason for producing the Critical Companion was 'to bring home to the widest possible audience the glaring inadequacies which recent research has exposed in the traditional Western account as well as in Soviet orthodoxy.' This is reflected in the themes chosen, which accord considerable importance to social, cultural and institutional history, and in the scholars dealing with them. At the same time the Critical Companion is pluralistic, featuring different approaches and interpretations by writers with widely different backgrounds and approaches. All are well qualified specialists in the spheres with which they deal. Western contributors enjoying an international reputation include, along with the British and American editors, Robert Daniels, Alexander Rabinowitch, Orlando Figes, Israel Getzler, Robert Service, Steve Smith, Dominic Lieven and the late Allan Wildman.

In the treatment of the controversial figure of Trotsky by Russian editor Vladimir Cherniaev we see a former Soviet historian seeking to overcome the demonology which characterised all references to Trotsky in the USSR between 1927 and 1987. He provides a competent account of Trotsky's career, recognising him as 'a key figure in the Russian revolution and Soviet state.' He balances his acknowledgement of Trotsky's very considerable reponsibility for the victory of the Red Army in the civil war by pointing to his equal responsibility for 'the establishment of a one-party authoritarian state with its apparatus for ruthlessly suppressing dissent'. This is undoubtedly true. However he does not indicate how far Trotsky went later, when in exile, in counterposing a pluralism of Soviet parties to a one-party state. He is likewise unfair in presenting Trotsky's *Literature and Revolution*, which specifically repudiated 'proletarian culture' and a party line on competing artistic schools, as a forerunner of Zhdanov's cultural conformism after World War II. Cherniaev recognises the need for developing a more profound understanding of Trotsky and obtaining access to relevant documents in those Russian archives which are still closed to researchers. The fact that there is little in his entry that will be unfamiliar to readers of Deutscher's Trotsky trilogy completed 35 years ago indicates the extent of the work that still needs to be undertaken by Russian historians. When can we hope to see the major critical biography of Trotsky by a fellow-countryman/woman which breaks substantial new groung and which, like that of Lenin, is long overdue? (Neither the opportunistic work by Volkogonov, despite the sole access to secret party archives that he enjoyed, nor that of the official Soviet Trotskyism 'expert' Vasetskii comes anywhere near to meeting the bill.)

Nikolai Smirnov, like Cherniaev from St. Petersburg, tells the 'tragic' story of the Constituent Assembly, elected by universal suffrage in November 1917. He concludes that its dissolution by the Lenin's government in January 1918 had as 'inevitable consequences ... the one-party monopoly of power,' and 'the state control of all social life'. It may however be argued that the dissolution of the Constituent Assembly was a stage in a process that was to lead step by step to the undemocratic consequences described, rather than of itself making them 'inevitable'.

The Critical Companion successfully achieves its editors' intention of providing the best of contemporary knowledge along with 'the agenda for future research'. It is an authoritative work of reference as well as setting the stage for wider co-operation between Western and Russian historians opening up perspectives for the history of the future. A Russian edition is planned. Although the volume's price will unfortunately limit individual purchase, it is an essential book for every library used by those seeking information and research leads on events and ideas which did so much to shape the history of this century.

Monty Johnstone
Monty Johnstone has written extensively on Soviet affairs and history

The general staff of the world revolution

Tim Rees and Andrew Thorpe (eds), *International Communism and the Communist International 1919–43* (Manchester University Press, 1998), 323pp., ISBN 0 7190 5116 9, £45.00 hbk, ISBN 0 7190 5546 6, £15.99 pbk.

Following the October Revolution in 1917 the Soviet government decided that the only way to safeguard their Bolshevik revolution was to extend it throughout Europe and the rest of the world. The instrument of this was to be the Communist International—or Comintern—established in March 1919: communist parties subsequently established in other countries were national sections of the World Party, with the Comintern as the central party apparatus and arbiter of policy for the whole organization. This collection of essays, based on the Third Medlicott Symposium, held at Exeter in 1995, examines the relationship between that centre and the 'national sections', and one of the most important questions addressed is how much influence and control the Comintern exerted over these individual communist parties. The eighteen contributors represent a diversity of opinion which could be said to echo the diverse experience of the parties discussed here and, not surprisingly, do not always come to the same conclusion on this key question. While each chapter can be read as a stand-alone study, taken together they form a very useful comparative collection. In addition, many are based on the Moscow archives that became available for the first time in the late 1980s, giving scope for new interpretations and insights.

The collection falls into three parts. In Part I, 'the view from the centre', David Kirby gives an analysis of the establishment of the Comintern and questions some of the accepted ideas on the permanent division of the left, charting the role of the Zimmerwald movement and the pressures exerted by the Great War and conflicting national interests and loyalties. Kevin McDermott looks at how the newly-available archival material has enlarged our understanding of the Comintern and concludes that no radically new interpretations are emerging, but that details and nuances in specialist areas will add depth to existing knowledge. McDennott's thoughts on the Comintern Archive are borne out by the third chapter in this section, in which Peter Huber uses the archive to produce, as far as possible within the limitations of available material, an analysis of the structure of the Moscow apparatus and its decision-making processes. These three chapters lay the foundations for the rest of the book.

Part II deals with the European parties and Part III with the American and Asian parties. There are tremendously different accounts of how much autonomy each national party exercised. Tim Rees argues that the Spanish communists during the civil war, while following Comintern guidelines, never did anything that they would not have done independently. In his conclusion he speaks of the 'power of the myth' of Comintern control from Moscow (p.161), and this phraseology is echoed by Andrew Thorpe writing on the British party. By contrast, Gerrit Voerman's study of Dutch communism in the 1920s chronicles the process whereby the Comintern completely undermined the autonomy of the Communist Party in the Netherlands. Having predated the Russian Revolution and enjoyed an independent existence for ten years before joining the Comintern, by 1930 the Dutch party was totally subordinate to Moscow. Guillaume Bourgeois uses biographical sketches from the archives to shed new light on the French Communist Party and some of the murkier goings on, identifying 'submission, autonomy, agents, conspiracy ... [as] ... keywords ... in relation to international communism between the wars' (p.101). Aleksandr Valtin's study of the Comintern archive reveals how much of the German revolution was planned in Moscow in 1923. It was the Russian Politburo that issued the directive to start the revolution and then cancelled it too late to prevent the bloody rising in Hamburg. He asserts that Moscow's constant interference in the KPD and attempts to balance left and right led to instability while giving KPD opponents the opportunity to accuse it of being under Moscow's control. Sandra Wilson challenges the idea that the Japanese party was blindly obedient to Moscow and throws light on some of the complexities facing Japanese communists, both within their own society and in relation to the Comintern's perception of them.

While opinions vary on the degree and extent of control, a consensus seems to emerge that the basic policies which emanated from the Comintern were, in general, adhered to by all the parties. From this, quite pronounced themes emerge as the parties adapt their domestic strategies to changing policy lines from the centre while coping with the effects these changes had on party unity and levels of popular support. All the chapters cover at least one of these major shifts, beginning with the retreat from overt revolutionary activity and Lenin's exhortations to form united front with reformist working-class parties in 1921. The next major challenge was the expulsion of Trotsky from the Comintern in 1927, followed by Stalin's 'class against class' dictum as he sought to eradicate Trotsky's influence. This in turn was superseded by a return to the formation of a Popular Front with other leftist elements in the mid 1930s as the fascist threat became ever more evident. Perhaps most difficult of all was the line put out following the signing of the Nazi-Soviet pact in August 1939, and the switch from anti-fascism to the concept that the democracies were only fighting the Nazis to safeguard their imperialist interests. This caused mixed feelings, but reactions were not so diverse when the line changed again—swiftly and radically—following the German invasion of the Soviet Union in June 1941.

Leading on from the various communist parties' attempts to cope with the complexities of policy changes the inescapable fact emerges—possibly voiced most strongly by Vatlin in relation to Germany, but certainly evident in many others—that the Comintern's policy-making was dominated by the needs of Soviet foreign policy. Those needs were pursued regardless of the interests of individual sections of the World Party—sometimes even to their detriment and sometimes seemingly against the basic *raison d'être* of the Comintern itself. Thus we see the Comintern advocating popular front, rather than revolutionary, tactics in Spain in 1937 as part of Stalin's need to further the alliance with Western democracies. Again, in Yugoslavia Tito was told to tone down his revolutionary rhetoric: first to avoid provoking the Nazis and then—following the German invasion of the USSR—for fear of upsetting Stalin's Western Allies. Ironically, given the fact that throughout its existence the Comintern had signally failed to spread revolution beyond the boundaries of Soviet Union, in the chapter on Yugoslavia Geoffrey Swain argues that the dissolution of the Comintern in 1943 was precisely the factor that allowed Tito and his partisans to complete their revolution. The Soviet Union dissolved the Comintern as a gesture of goodwill towards the Western Allies to encourage the latter to open the longed-for second front and take some of the heat off the Red Army. In a further irony, angst about the delayed second front was an important element in the British decision to support Tito and his communist resistance movement as a means of diverting German troops from the Eastern front: this support was not unhelpful in furthering the Yugoslav revolution. Swain also points out that Tito had learned the lesson of Spain: not for him the policy of the Popular Front, his success hinged upon ensuring complete communist dominance in any 'coalition'.

Why did the Comintern fail to export revolution? The editors point out that this was a very difficult task to begin with, and this collection of essays provides fascinating insights into many of the factors that made it an impossible one. Rees argues that Comintern influence in Spain was blunted by a lack of clear-cut up to date information: in a fast moving and potentially revolutionary situation the attempt at central control by a slow moving bureaucratic organisation was doomed from the outset. Much the same point emerges from Barry Carr's essay on Cuba. It is a good collection for students of Communism in general, for those who want to make comparisons between regions which specially interest them, and for those who want to just dip in and see what details and nuances are available in the light of new sources.

Heather Williams
Heather Williams teaches at Southampton University and is a member of the Socialist History editorial team

Mystery man

R. Darlington, *The Political Trajectory of J. T. Murphy* (Liverpool University Press, Liverpool, 1998), 316pp., ISBN 0 85323 743 3, £32.00 hbk.

M. Murphy, *Molly Murphy: Suffragette and Socialist*, with an introduction by Ralph Darlington (Salford: Institute of Social Research, University of Salford, 1998), 316pp, ISBN 0 904483 25 8.

John Thomas Murphy became nationally known as a leader of the shop steward's movement during and immediately after the First World War. From his base in the Sheffield engineering industry he sought to theorise shop steward power in *The Workers' Committee* (1917). In common with other talented militants of the day, who shared the distinction of having made independent efforts to find an alternative to bureaucratised trade unionism and an electoral politics that seemed to be going nowhere, Murphy was converted to Bolshevism. His industrial background and journalistic abilities were put to use as a founder member of the Communist Party of Great Britain (CPGB) in which he served as a Central Committee member with special responsibility for the party's industrial work and as editor of its theoretical journal *Communist Review*. Murphy's early visits to Moscow brought him to the attention of Lenin and he was selected to help launch the Red International of Labour Unions (Profintern) and served on the Presidium of the Executive Committee of the Communist International. Murphy belonged to that large group of foreign Communists who admired Stalin; he even moved the resolution to expel Trotsky from the Executive Committee of the Comintern (ECCI). But he was alone among the British Communist leaders in resigning from the Party he had helped to fashion. After his abrupt departure from the organisation in 1932 he turned to the Socialist League, a left-wing ginger group inside the Labour Party. Long before his death in 1965, however, Murphy had grown disillusioned with politics. Strangely for one so fond of writing, he was silent about the Communist experience to an extraordinary degree.

According to Ralph Darlington, 'the problem for Murphy, was that in rejecting the critique of Stalinism presented by Trotsky and his supporters, he had no alternative theoretical and practical basis from which to assess his negative experience in the Communist Party other than through the prism of left reformism'. This does not seem to me to be a very convincing explanation of Murphy's diffidence. Murphy had a wealth of experience at his disposal. He had been admitted to virtually all levels of the Communist movement, his background in trade unionism and the Socialist Labour Party had acquainted him with syndicalist, guild socialist and pre-Bolshevik Marxist ideas and he inhabited a world which was fascinated by the Soviet Union. Cogent analyses of Stalinism—some of them written by socialists and former Communists—were available—witness Anton Ciliga's *The Russian Enigma* (1940). 'Inside information', which Murphy could have reviewed and elaborated on, was provided by the likes of Krivitsky, Victor Serge, Alexander Barmine, Louis Fischer, Buber-Neumann, Dallin and Nicolaevsky during the same decade.

Murphy's defection from the CPGB is especially curious because it came after a long period during which he took his colleagues to task for not being Communist enough. He wanted sterner critiques of the left trade union leaders after the general strike; he wanted a sharper leftward turn from the Party in its application of the Third Period line; he wanted the Party to agitate for non-payment of the trade unions' political levy to the Labour Party; in short he was the most ultra of the ultra-lefts. True, he criticised Dutt's rendition of the 'decaying Labour Party' mantra in 1931—though he had chanted in harmony with his colleagues up to that point and even a little louder than most of them. But as late in his Party career as 1931 he criticised Dutt only because he wanted to intensify the CP's fight against Labour. The actual break from the Party was occasioned by a very minor issue. The Party leadership repudiated Murphy's argument that the CP should campaign for trade between Britain and the Soviet Union—an old argument that had been quite the thing before Stalin launched the ultra-left turn of 1928. When Murphy resigned rather than publicly admit his 'errors', Pollitt and Co. announced that he had been expelled from the Party. Publicly he was branded as a Trotskyist; privately his defection was explained in crude material terms—Murphy, it was said, could not afford to remain in the Party.

In 1928 Murphy and his wife Molly had decided to send their son Gordon to Bedales private boarding school. This inevitably provoked the disapproval of their comrades. When Murphy lost his job as London correspondent of

Pravda just months before his resignation from the Party an important source of income dried up. His lifestyle may also have suffered from the decision—taken, again, just weeks before the resignation dispute began—to transfer him from the London headquarters to Sheffield; Molly's reflections certainly leave no doubt that they found life in the capital to their satisfaction.

The argument that led to Murphy's resignation was so trivial, that his domestic circumstances may well have been a major part of the cause. Perhaps Murphy also realised that his upward trajectory in the Party was blocked, despite his best efforts to find a distinctive spin for his loyal support of Comintern policy. To all outward appearance Murphy nevertheless remained a Stalinist through and through during the 1930s. He continued to call himself a 'revolutionary marxist', he saw the danger of fascism in Britain coming from much the same quarters as those that his former comrades indicated—in the National Government, in the trend to a corporate state, in any 'Roosevelt Recovery Plans' for Britain; he repudiated the idea that socialism could come through Parliament, but believed that socialism was the only thing that would stop fascism. In all these things he mimicked Dutt and Pollitt. He continued to 'defend' the Soviet Union, seeing it as the best defence against fascism, believing earnestly that it was building socialism. He campaigned for the building of Popular Fronts to promote an alliance with Soviet Russia. He was apparently unconcerned by the Moscow Trials and defended the Hitler-Stalin pact. Though he criticised Russia's invasion of Finland his hagiography of Stalin, published in 1945, showed that his pro-Soviet outlook was little changed and he justified the dictator's violent transformation of Russia in the name of progress and civilization.

Up until this point Murphy's only persuasive explanation for his break from the CPGB had been contained in *Preparing For Power* (1934) where he suggested that the Party had been still-born in Britain and only functioned as a sectarian nuisance, when it would have been better for revolutionary socialists to have operated as the left wing of the Labour Party. But then this was precisely what the Socialist League was purportedly doing at the time, and Murphy was making a living as its London organiser and contributing to its monthly journal. The case he made against the Communist Party in 1934 was self-serving, and in no way represents Murphy's coming to terms with the Leninist-Stalinist project.

Ralph Darlington came upon Molly Murphy's story while researching *The Political Trajectory* and he must have felt a thrill of anticipation when he first began to read the unpublished manuscript. It seems to have been written by J. T. Murphy but is assumed to be an authentic expression of Molly's own account of her life and is dated from the early 1960s. Molly was working as an organiser for the Women's Social and Political Union when she first met Murphy in 1913, but was thirty years old by the time they married and headed for Soviet Russia in early 1921. In the Hotel Lux they met a galaxy of Communist leaders. On their return to Britain Molly joined the Party herself. After the general strike they went back to Russia for 18 months while Jack served on the ECCI. The big names of the movement appear again in Molly's telling of the tale but no light is shed on their personalities and politics. A strange unreality pervades the manuscript because it is rarely much more than a travelogue written by someone who has reason to think that they have led an interesting life but for lack of something—ideas? courage?—is unable to find the words to bring it alive on the page. A rare exception is a passage in which Molly recounts the story of a young American blinded in the Spanish civil war whom she nursed in a hospital on the Madrid front. But the error-strewn, micoscopic print of this published memoir, reveals nothing about the CPGB, the Comintern, or Bolshevik Russia.

Jack Murphy dropped out of politics after the war, Molly had a breakdown in 1942 and their son Gordon—who received the education they were both denied—qualified as a doctor in 1944. During the 1950s wealthy friends such as Alan Sainsbury (the grocer) helped the Murphys financially and enabled them to live in an attractive semi-detached in Highgate. According to a rare article of this period, published in *Peace News* in December 1956, Murphy had become disillusioned with both Marxism and the USSR by 1953. Marxism and Leninism he saw now as 'a mixture of mythology and oversimplified theories of history, harnessed to a militaristic party of social conquest for the establishment of its own militaristic dictatorship'. In 1958 he added (in the *New Reasoner*) that religious faith had dominated reason among the first generation of British Leninists and that the Communist Party had become more interested in defending doctrine than changing society. There is obviously something in these reflections but it is a poor harvest from the worker-intellectual who had spent a lifetime in socialist politics. This is a man who had lived in the USSR and known the leaders of the Comintern and the CPGB. He had once famously dissected the workings of (trade union) organisations. Murphy was only twelve years a Communist, but he was perhaps thirty years a Stalinist. Why? How was that possible?

Darlington, alas, was unable to find anything that would shed much light on such questions. Though his research is thorough and involved talking to Murphy's surviving family in Canada, Darlington hasn't turned up anything new. His text is punctuated with observations concerned with Murphy's ideological errors and shortcomings, but these invariably consist of deviations from Darlington's conception of the true path—which happens to be SWP-Bolshevism. This rather limits the nature of his enquiry, I think, and the combination of familiar facts with ready-made questions and answers makes for pretty dull fare. Murphy's life, after Darlington's efforts, still consists of the things that that first became familiar through the work of L. J. Macfarlane, James Hinton, and others.

John Callaghan
John Callaghan has written extensively on the Communist and Trotskyist movements

Culture and the future that never was

Andy Croft (ed.), *A Weapon in the Struggle: The cultural history of the Communist Party in Britain* (Pluto Press, London, 1998), viii + 218pp., ISBN 0 7453 1204 7, £14.99 pbk.

David Margolies (ed.), *Writing the Revolution: Cultural criticism from* Left Review (Pluto Press, London, 1998), ix + 208pp., ISBN 0 7453 1162 8, £12.99 pbk.

J. Hoberman, *The Red Atlantis: Communist culture in the absence of communism* (Temple University Press, Philadelphia, USA, 1998), 314pp., ISBN 1 5663 9643 3, $34.95 hbk.

The publication of *Questions of Ideology and Culture* by the CPGB's Executive Committee in 1967 was seen as a watershed in the Party's attempts to break with dogmatism and reductionism in its relationship to arts and culture. The Party went to pains to clarify its commitment to pluralism. 'We welcome', it announced, 'the widest variety of artistic approaches, subjects and styles, and encourage our members freely to express their views.' In a period in which the Cold War was losing its grip, new possibilities were opening up for Communist-Christian dialogue and the Party itself was hoping to find a new generation of intellectuals, the concern was to avoid the impression of demanding a Party line on the direction of art and culture, the superiority of Soviet art forms, simple polarities between 'bourgeois' and 'proletarian' culture, or the view that only under socialism could meaningful artistic expression take place. The subsequent discussion in *Marxism Today* and other sections of the Party press confirmed that 'contradictory' currents were still prevalent in the Party on these questions, with members in turn welcoming the 'humanistic', 'anti-dogmatic' approach, as well as the 'lead' given towards a higher culture by the socialist countries. The need for individual autonomy was argued side-by-side with complaints that intellectuals had become 'isolated' from the wider community. The need to avoid reducing art to politics was asserted alongside calls for more ideological and political direction.

However, as these collections by Croft and Margolies show, such tensions were neither new, nor should they obscure the originality, commitment to a breadth of cultural endeavours, and the socialist humanism of Party intellectuals and cultural workers. As Andy Croft says in the introduction to his ground-breaking, if inevitably eclectic collection, 'the arts were were one of the ways in which Communist ideas entered the mainstream of British life and through which the Party was able to identify itself as the defender of native, popular traditions and as the bearer of the new, and therefore of the future'. Thus in the pre-1956 period (largely the focus of this collection), we find Communists in the thick of the avant-garde through the graphic art of the 'the three James's' (Boswell, Fitton, and Holland) in the thirties; making a significant contribution to 'highbrow' culture of classical music as well as helping to break down the 'high-low' cultural division, for example in the development of the 'progressive' song and the 'mass historical dramas' of the working-class pageant. One of these brought 78,000 (the size of a Cup Final crowd) to the *Towards Tommorow* event held at Wembley in July 1938. These are all covered in Croft's collection, while David Margolies has put together a selection of work first published in *Left Review* in the 1930s, a journal which the collection's blurb claims was the first in the field of cultural studies, and the first indication that Marxist critical theory had grown up.

Socialist humanism was a key feature in the upsurge of communist art and culture. First it asserted that literature and art were essential parts of life, that a democratic culture was an essential part of the means as well as the ends of socialism, and that access and participation to cultural life needed to be extended. It was also hostile to commercial and 'decadent' forms of British and American culture, often at this time comparing them unfavourably with Soviet culture as well as with alternative popular working-class forms. The Party had voted at its 1952 Congress to reject the 'Americanisation of Britain's cultural life' and its 'reactionary films and debased literature and comics', while the American dance routines of the late 1940's were seen as 'decadent, yankee be-bop'. 'Jitterbugging', according to the young British communists discussed by Kevin Morgan in his chapter on jazz, 'is really the lowest to which anyone can sink. To turn oneself into a slobbering savage, a drooling, psychopathic horror, a jerking bundle of sensual emotions.'

Culture and politics

Above all, as the titles of the two books of essays indicate, it was the commitment to politics that distinguished the Communist contribution to culture, and though many would not have been overly disappointed that 'the Party never had a coherent or effective policy towards the political song' (as Gerald Porter put it), intellectuals were expected to pull their political weight in their cultural work. This was apparent in the growth of the Artists International, the Writers International and the Workers Music Association, all formed in the Popular Front era against the background of the Spanish Civil War and the fascist threat. This marked a break with 'class against class' reductionism, even if support for the Soviet Union was regarded as an informal membership requirement for some of these organisations. Zhdanov and Lysenko were always lurking in the background, and reductionism remained with some contributors to *Left Review*. Alec Brown, for example, wanted 'the proletarianisation of our outlook and language', seeing the purpose of writing with only 'one end in view, the revolutionary end of establishing a socialist republic.' Yet, as an early Writers International statement argued, it was important to be for both 'militant Communism and … individualism and metaphysics in the Arts'. The pursuit of individual artistic expression and political liberation, therefore, were not held to be mutually exclusive.

Of course, there were those in the communist movement who could not resolve some of these contradictions. Alan Bush, the British composer who was one of the most prominent of the Party's cultural figures, is considered by Hanlon and Waite in their chapter. They argue that he could not—particularly in his later work—escape the constraints of the Soviet orthodoxy he had internalised. This resulted in the paradox of 'Shostakovich…sticking his neck out in the Soviet Union, with such musically and politically challenging works as the songs based on Jewish folk poetry (while) Bush was setting leftish doggerel to simple folk tunes in the context of a (national) political culture which would have allowed him to explore the many interesting musical worlds which his earliest pieces had hinted at'.

Such contradictions also feature in J. Hoberman's journey into the world of Jewish-American communism, an even more eclectic set of essays which stands as a good companion to Raphael Samuel's 'Lost World of British Communism' articles in *New Left Review* in the mid-1980s. Hoberman's 'lost world' contains a fascinating mix of cultural legacies ranging from Socialist

Realist painting, Soviet Jewish cinema, Victor Serge and the Rosenbergs, to the Berlin Wall, to which he attributes a particularly original cultural significance. 'The Wall was itself a work of art. It belongs with the never-built Palace of the Soviets, the Jewish autonomous oblast of Birobidzhan, Franz Kafka's posthumous career as a dissident writer…and the wreckage of communist fantasy itself, submerged now in History's secret depths.'

Geoff Andrews
Geoff Andrews is completing his PhD on the 'Culture, Ideology and Strategy of the CPGB 1968–1979', and was co-editor of Opening the Books: Essays on the social and cultural history of British communism
(Pluto Press, London, 1995)

Books Received

Reviews of some of the following items are in preparation and will appear in future issues of the journal. Publishers sending items to be considered for review, and readers interested in reviewing any of the publications listed here, should write to Kate Duffy, *Socialist History* assistant reviews editor, University of Luton, Park Square, Luton LU1 3JU. Kate's e-mail address is: kate.duffy@luton.ac.uk

Readers considering submitting articles other than reviews, or sending general correspondence, should write to the *Socialist History* editorial team care of Kevin Morgan, Department of Government, University of Manchester, M13 9PL. His e-mail address is kevin.morgan@man.ac.uk

Patrick Pasture and Johan Verberckmoes (eds), *Working Class Internationalism and the Appeal of National Identity: historical debates and current perspectives an Western Europe* (Berg, Oxford, 1998), vii + 263pp., ISBN 1 8597 3281, £44.99 hbk.

Caroline Kennedy-Pipe, *Russia and the World 1917–1991* (Arnold, London, 1998), x + 229pp., ISBN 0 3406 5205 5, £13.99 pbk.

Stephen Roberts and Dorothy Thompson, *Images of Chartism* (Merlin Press, Rendlesham, 1998) vi + 110pp., ISBN 0 8503 6475 2, £12.95 pbk.

Ernie Trory, *Peace and the Cold War: part two: The crucial years: 1952–60* (Crabtree Press, Hove, 1998), 288pp., ISBN 0 9515 0961, £9.50 pbk.

Marc Wadsworth, *Comrade Sak: Shapurji Saklatvala MP: A political biography* (Peepal Press, 17 Kings Avenue, Leeds, 1998), 202pp., ISBN 0 9488 3377 7, £9.99 pbk.

Chris Williams, *Capitalism, Community and Conflict the South Wales Coalfield 1898–1947* (University of Wales Press, *The Past In Perspective* series, Cardiff, 1998), xvi + 146pp., ISBN 0 7083 1473 2, £7.99 pbk.

Conference Report

One of the most imaginative academic conference series of recent years has begun exploring the ways in which conceptions of alternative futures motivate people involved in social movements. Here we present an account by one of the organisers, and comments from an Irish participant.

Any reader interested in the conferences can contact Mike Tyldesley at the Department of Politics and Philosophy, Manchester Metropolitan University, Geoffrey Manton Building, Rosamund Street West, Oxford Road, Manchester, M15 6LL. e-mail: M.Tyldesley@mmu.ac.uk

Some volumes of the papers from previous conferences may be available through Mike Tyldesley. A review of a published collection of papers from the first 'Alternative Futures and Popular Protest', conference appeared in the last issue of *Socialist History*.

Alternative Futures and Popular Protest
Mike Tyldesley

Alternative Futures and Popular Protest is the name of what has become a continuing series of conferences that take place around Easter-time at the Manchester Metropolitan University. The first in the series happened in 1995, and there have been subsequent conferences every year since.

What do the conferences focus on? At a general level this is fairly easy to state. The popular protest aspect of the title can be seen as referring to the general field of Social Movements—perhaps this is the side that Colin is more concerned with—and the alternative futures aspect to ideas for new ways of structuring society—and, again, perhaps this is more my focus. However, the obvious point is that really the two go together in ways that often mean that such a division is rather artificial and it only serves to point out emphases in the debates and discussion rather than hard-and-fast divisions of subject matter.

This general statement is fairly schematic. In practical terms it has resulted in a very wide-ranging series of conferences, which have seen themes emerge and run from year to year. Issues that might be picked out include the theoretical understanding of social movements and protest activity, current eco-activism such as the roads protest movements, third world social and protest movements, and utopian projects. However, it must be said that picking such themes out does give the full flavour of conferences that have a wide variety of topics discussed at them.

At the fourth conference, easter 1998, there were presentations on—inter alia—the thinking of Hakim Bey, the Liverpool Docks dispute, anti-vaccination campaigns in Britain between 1867 and 1910, the Exodus Collective, the Irish Women's Movement, Woody Guthrie, Amilcar Cabral and Walter Rodney, the New German Right, Spiritual Feminism and New Age Politics, Social Movements in Latin America, two papers on community struggles in Glasgow, and many more.

This may suggest a confusing eclecticism. Such a response would be incorrect, in that the overall theme of the conferences is one that enables people with a wide variety of interests to meet and get into useful discussions. The conferences are pulled together by approach rather than immediate subject matter.

Three further points could be made regarding the intellectual content of the conferences. The first, and perhaps most important, is that there is no privileging of the academic voice as against the non-academic. The conferences have all seen significant papers from participants in some of the movements they describe. In some cases such contributions have come from academics, in some cases from non-academics. The issue of whether one works as an academic or not only really impacts on the conference in the sense that it is usually easier for academics to get funding to attend conferences like the Alternative Futures and Popular Protest series. This is actually a major disadvantage for all concerned. We would like to see more voices from outside the academy.

No party line

The second point is to note that there is no specific 'line' of analysis laid down in advance by the organisers. The subject matter of the conference does mean that there is a tendency for people with interests in generally 'left' topics and ideas to wish to present papers. Within this category there have been contributions from Marxists, Anarchists, Utopian Socialists and others. Additionally, there have been presentations about subjects falling outside the usual areas of left concern, and also from people connected with sections of the green movement that would perhaps be wary of being labelled 'left'. So there are no dogmas being imposed. There are vigorous and sometimes heated debates.

The third point is that the conference is 'multi-disciplinary'. Our academic contributors have come from a wide variety of disciplines, from Politics, Sociology and History to Architecture and Anthropology. For some of us, this could be seen as a useful reminder that the departmental boundaries in the academic world can sometimes get in the way of useful research, rather than facilitate it. In the era of the so-called Research Assessment Exercise in higher education, an important point to be borne in mind.

How are the conferences organised? At a formal level, they consist of eight sets of sessions spread over three days (an afternoon, a full day and a morning), with two or sometimes three sessions running simultaneously. A typical session would see two presenters of related papers each with 20 minutes or so to outline their papers, with 30 to 40 minutes discussion of each paper. We do ask participants to send their papers in to us in advance of the conference, so that on registration the participants receive a couple of books of papers. This saves the scrambling around for papers that sometimes goes on at conferences, makes it easy to ensure that participants don't mislay that vital paper that often seems to get lost on the way home, and it also means that often discussion can proceed on the basis of informed comment. We frequently find that participants in sessions that particularly interest them have read the speakers' papers prior to the session. We'd like to think—and have been told—that this contributes to sessions that are useful for both the presenters and their audience.

There are no plenary sessions. We experimented with plenaries featuring a couple of 'big names' at the first conference, and they did not really contribute to the conference sufficiently to justify continuing with the idea. The plenaries at these conferences actually take place in the less formal sessions of the conference. These consist of gatherings for meals and in the pub. The conference has a 'formal' meal within the university on one evening, and a less formal session is arranged for the second evening. A pub near to the venue is usually 'adopted' for the duration of the conference, and its here and at the meals and coffee breaks that the real plenaries happen. These are, of course, the debates and discussions that continue the themes addressed in the sessions.

A participant's comments
Laurence Cox

The annual AFFP conference is the only regular academic conference on social movements in general in Britain. Ireland has none. This makes it something of a mecca for researchers in these islands. It brings together a variety of disciplines, from architects to philosophers, along with the more predictable historians, sociologists, etc; various areas of interest including labour history, dance culture, 'spiritual feminism' and the New Right; and a range of approaches.

This makes participation quite a mental stretch, and extremely challenging. I have yet to meet anyone who felt they were wasting their time there. What makes it work is obviously the interest in a shared object, but also, I suspect, the sense that the answers matter sufficiently to risk the kind of communication and rethinking that's involved. The success of the conference depends on the fact that a high proportion of the regulars—but also I think of the new faces—are themselves actively involved in the things they're writing about, and so have common experiences over and above the specific issues and theories they are themselves committed to.

Despite the disparity, there does seen to be a politics to the conference, albeit shifting its ground over time. The 1997 and 1996 conferences struck me as being centred around a 'critical discussion', friendly but serious, between Marxist analyses and overtly class-related themes on the one hand, and a more disparate set of analyses geared to the radical ecology movement, rave culture and so on on the other.

In 1998, with 'New Labour' firmly in the saddle, discussion seemed perhaps a bit less focused, but the general theme of a creative tension or engagement between an open-minded Marxism on the one hand and on the other a range of theories (from feminism and anarchism to cultural studies and theories of language) with more appeal for activists in contemporary movements or more pull in the contemporary academy remains to me at least one of the most attractive and characteristic features of the conferences.

SUBSCRIBE TO SOCIALIST HISTORY

Annual subscription for individuals is £15 waged, £10 unwaged and £25 to overseas members. Send subscription with name and address to:
>Secretary,
Socialist History Society,
6 Cynthia Street,
London N1 9JF

Institutional and library subscription is £25 per annum. Send requests to:
>Subscriptions,
Rivers Oram Press,
144 Hemingford Road,
London N1 1DE